To

_____

From

_____

Date

_____

POWER PRAYERS

FOR BOYS

GLENN HASCALL

SHILOH ♪ kidz

An Imprint of Barbour Publishing, Inc.

© 2015 by Barbour Publishing, Inc.

Written by Emily Biggers and Glenn Hascall

Print ISBN 978-1-63058-858-8

eBook Editions:
Adobe Digital Edition (.epub) 978-1-63409-296-8
Kindle and MobiPocket Edition (.prc) 978-1-63409-297-5

Published by Shiloh Kidz, an imprint of Barbour Publishing, Inc., P.O. Box 719, Uhrichsville, Ohio 44683, www.shilohkidz.com

Our mission is to publish and distribute inspirational products offering exceptional value and biblical encouragement to the masses.

ecpa Member of the
Evangelical Christian
Publishers Association

Printed in the United States of America.
05016 0315 DP

CONTENTS

INTRODUCTION

God's Word is filled with praise, prayer, promises, and perspective. You can learn what God says and then let Him know You understand through prayer. That's why you're here.

Spend a few minutes grappling with things that are important to God. You'll discover what God has to say about purity, service, forgiveness, pride, and bullying. Each prayer can help you let God know you understand what He says. These verses and prayers will also encourage you to do more than just say words. Taking action always follows understanding truth.

We hope you're serious about following Him. Be prepared to encounter God's wise words, work through helpful prayers, and make wise decisions for your future based on what you discover.

God wants to have a conversation with you. His words and your prayers help you understand that He really understands your struggles.

Are you ready to start this unexpected adventure?

MY ATTITUDE—
THE POWER OF MY THOUGHTS

School hallways often display posters that make statements about attitude. They may say things such as Attitude Is Everything or Attitude Is a Small Thing That Makes a BIG Difference! Do you believe this? It is amazing how much of a difference your attitude truly can make. Focusing on the things that bring you down can really make for a bad day. When you are down, try focusing on God's truth about you. He knit you together in your mother's womb. He has plans for your future that are good, not bad. These truths from the Bible can change your attitude and make for a better day all the way around. Ask God to help you improve your attitude. He is honored when your attitude reflects a thankful heart.

You must have the same attitude that Christ Jesus had.
Though he was God, he did not think of equality with God as
something to cling to. Instead, he gave up his divine privileges;
he took the humble position of a slave and was born as a human being.
PHILIPPIANS 2:5—7 NLT

Lord, make me more like Jesus. He is humble and kind. He does
not flaunt His status as Your Son. When he lived on earth, he
walked among the people as a teacher and friend. He led by
example. My parents and teachers speak of being a good leader,
leading others in a positive way. Help me to be that kind of person
with an attitude like Christ's. Help me to love those around me
and to be humble even if I am praised by adults or friends. Thank
You for helping me. Amen.

You were taught to leave your old self—to stop living the evil way you lived before. That old self becomes worse, because people are fooled by the evil things they want to do. But you were taught to be made new in your hearts, to become a new person. That new person is made to be like God—made to be truly good and holy.

EPHESIANS 4:22–24 NCV

Lord, in You I am a new person. I don't have to be my old self. Sin is so easy to get tangled up in, but You free me from my old ways of thinking. Fill my mind with Your goodness and Your ways. Help me to be a new person. Your Word says that I am a new creation in Christ. Help me to live like a new creation, not like a lost soul who is sad and depressed. Put a smile in my heart that I might bring You glory today in my attitude and in my actions. Amen.

* * * * * * * *

May the God who gives endurance and encouragement give you the same attitude of mind toward each other that Christ Jesus had, so that with one mind and one voice you may glorify the God and Father of our Lord Jesus Christ.

ROMANS 15:5–6 NIV

Heavenly Father, I want to include others. I don't want to be the person who divides; I want to be someone who brings people together. Sometimes I get caught up in wanting to hang out with just a certain group of people. I forget about others. At times I even treat them coldly. Make my attitude more like the attitude Jesus had when He walked on earth. He included. He built unity. He did not divide. I want to have this type of mind-set. Help me, Lord. Amen.

A cheerful heart is good medicine,
but a crushed spirit dries up the bones.
PROVERBS 17:22 NIV

Heavenly Father, I ask today that You would help me to have a cheerful heart. I know that laughter is good medicine. I don't like the taste of most medicines, to be honest, but I know that laughter is sweet! You delight in my laughter because I am Your precious child. You want me to be happy. You want me to have joy deep down in my heart, not just a temporary feeling. This kind of joy comes only through Jesus. Thank You for loving me! Amen.

* * * * * * * * *

Pride leads to destruction; a proud attitude brings ruin.
PROVERBS 16:18 NCV

Help me, God, to be humble. I know that pride in my heart is not a good thing. Your Word says it brings destruction. I want to be built up in You. I want to build others up, also. I do not want destruction in my life. Cause me to see others as important. Help me to remember that everyone around me has a struggle even if I can't see it on the outside. Help my attitude toward others to be kind and loving, not haughty or prideful. Amen.

For the Kingdom of God is not a matter of what we eat or drink,
but of living a life of goodness and peace and joy in the Holy Spirit.
If you serve Christ with this attitude, you will please God,
and others will approve of you, too.
ROMANS 14:17–18 NLT

Lord Jesus, make me a servant. I so often want to be in charge.
Remind me that You are the Lord of my life and that I am to serve
You with joy, peace, and goodness. These attitudes can be found
in me only if I allow the Holy Spirit to control me. I want to please
You and to serve You well. I want to serve others around me also
and to help them in any way I can. Amen.

* * * * * * * * *

Finally, all of you should be of one mind. Sympathize
with each other. Love each other as brothers and sisters.
Be tenderhearted, and keep a humble attitude.
1 PETER 3:8 NLT

God, it is hard to remember that other Christians are my brothers
and sisters. Just as I should treat my siblings with love and care,
I should do the same for my brothers and sisters in Christ. Give
me little reminders throughout my day today that we are all one
family. Help me to feel the hurt and see the needs of those around
me. Help me to love as You love—without condition. Amen.

Do everything without complaining and arguing,
so that no one can criticize you. Live clean, innocent lives
as children of God, shining like bright lights in a world
full of crooked and perverse people.
PHILIPPIANS 2:14–15 NLT

Jesus, so many times I am tempted to complain. I hear others doing it constantly, and I want to join in on the comments. "I hate homework" or "Why do I have to empty the trash every single day?" are words that flow off my tongue before I can even catch myself. Help me to take every thought to You before that thought becomes a complaint. Remind me of all of my blessings, and help me to cut down on the number of times I complain each day. I know You can help me to have a better attitude. Thank You, Lord. Amen.

> The father of godly children has cause for joy.
> What a pleasure to have children who are wise. So give your
> father and mother joy! May she who gave you birth be happy.
> PROVERBS 23:24–25 NLT

Heavenly Father, help me to have a good attitude at home. I know what it means to have good manners. I have been taught to treat adults with respect. When it comes to my own parents, it is sometimes hard. I find myself having a bad attitude when they ask me to do things. I want to bring my parents joy. I want to be a godly young person. Help me with this. It is a daily struggle, but I know I can find victory in You! Amen.

* * * * * * * * *

> "In your anger do not sin": Do not let the
> sun go down while you are still angry.
> EPHESIANS 4:26 NIV

Lord Jesus, I do get angry sometimes. You tell me in Your Word that anger is not a sin but that I should not let it lead to sin. Please help me to have a good attitude toward others around me even when I am angry. I don't want to take my anger out on other people. Give me the self-control I need to keep from sinning when I'm mad. Amen.

Don't use foul or abusive language. Let everything you say
be good and helpful, so that your words will be
an encouragement to those who hear them.
EPHESIANS 4:29 NLT

Dear God, how I want to be an encourager! I have teachers and
friends in my life who encourage me. They build me up with their
words. I feel good just being around them. Make me more like
these people. Jesus is an encourager. He encouraged and taught
His disciples. The Bible says He loved them. Fill my heart with
love for others and put in me a spirit of encouragement. In Jesus'
name. Amen.

* * * * * * * * *

Don't love money; be satisfied with what you have. For God has said,
"I will never fail you. I will never abandon you."
HEBREWS 13:5 NLT

Heavenly Father, You know my heart. You know all my thoughts—
the good ones and the not-so-good ones. I might as well admit that
I feel jealous at times. I see what others have, and I want it. I wish
my family had more money. Please remind me that this attitude is
not pleasing to You. Remind me that I have everything I need in
You. I do not want to have a jealous or greedy attitude. Thank You,
Lord. Amen.

My dear brothers and sisters, always be willing to listen
and slow to speak. Do not become angry easily.
JAMES 1:19 NCV

Dear Lord, make me a good listener. I am often too quick to try to
talk, talk, talk. People really just want a listening ear, not a quick
fix for their problems. I know that I feel valued and loved when
a family member or friend listens to me. Give me a kind attitude
toward anyone who comes to me to share their worries. May I be
loving, and may I avoid trying to fill every empty moment with my
own voice. Amen.

For the word of God is alive and active. Sharper than any double-edged sword, it penetrates even to dividing soul and spirit, joints and marrow; it judges the thoughts and attitudes of the heart. Nothing in all creation is hidden from God's sight. Everything is uncovered and laid bare before the eyes of him to whom we must give account.

HEBREWS 4:12–13 NIV

God, I know You see my attitude even when I try to hide it from others. You see my heart and know the way I feel. I want to please You with my thoughts. I want to be able to have a good attitude even when someone treats me wrongly or when I am disappointed. It is so hard! I can't do it alone, but Your Word says that I can do all things through Christ who gives me strength. Help me to have an attitude today that is pleasing to You. In Jesus' name I pray. Amen.

MY BIBLE—
THE POWER OF GOD'S WORD

The Bible is not like any other book. It is God's Holy Word. Every word on its pages was breathed by God and written down by men under His direction. The Bible is useful for teaching Christians how to live. It corrects our wrong thinking. It trains us in godliness. In the Bible we learn about doing good deeds in order to glorify our Father in heaven. It can provide great comfort and peace. In some places in the world today it is against the law to read and study the Bible. People hold secret church meetings and risk their lives to read the Bible. We should never take for granted our freedom to read God's Word in this country. Honor the Bible. Live by it. Teach it to others. God wants you to take His Word seriously.

Blessed is the one who does not walk in step with the wicked
or stand in the way that sinners take or sit in the company
of mockers, but whose delight is in the law of the LORD,
and who meditates on his law day and night.
PSALM 1:1–2 NIV

Dear God, I love to start and finish my day reading Your Word and meditating on it. Reveal to me the truths You want me to learn. Guide which verses I read each day so that You might teach me what I need to know that day. You are all-powerful, and You can show me things in Your Word. I trust You to instruct me as a teacher does a student. I want Your Word to be the first thing I put into my mind each day and the last thing I dwell on before I drift off to sleep. Amen.

Jesus answered, "It is written: 'Man shall not live on bread alone, but on every word that comes from the mouth of God.'"
MATTHEW 4:4 NIV

Jesus, when You were tempted by Satan, You told him that the Word of God sustained You. May it nourish my heart and soul just as food nourishes my body. I want to know the Bible so well that when I am found in tempting spots, I will be able to stand strong against the devil. I love the Word of God. May I show it through the amount of time I spend reading it versus all the other activities that try to crowd the Bible out of my schedule. Amen.

* * * * * * * * *

I will obey your demands, so please don't ever leave me.
PSALM 119:8 NCV

Help me, Lord, to follow Your ways. They are so clear in the Bible. I just need to read it and apply it to my life, but that is easier said than done. I want to honor You in the way I live. I know that I cannot keep Your law perfectly, and that is why You provided Jesus to die for my sins and make a way for me to be saved. Still, out of my great love for You, I want to live in a way that pleases You. Amen.

> **Until I come, continue to read the Scriptures to the people,
> strengthen them, and teach them.**
> 1 TIMOTHY 4:13 NCV

Dear Jesus, I know You are coming back one day. Until then, thank You that I have Your Word. It is here for me to learn from and to share with others. It is a guide for my life. Just as toys and electronics come with users' guides or instruction booklets, You have given me the Bible to live by until You come back for me. Thank You for Your Holy Word. Amen.

* * * * * * * * *

> **In the beginning there was the Word.
> The Word was with God, and the Word was God.**
> JOHN 1:1 NCV

God, You are eternal, and so is Your Word. It will last forever. I cherish the Bible and want to follow Your ways that You teach me on its pages. I know that Your Word is breathed by You and that it is written to teach me and correct me and guide me. Help me to treat it with respect and to memorize its teachings so that I might glorify You in how I live. Amen.

"I have not departed from the commands of his lips; I have treasured
the words of his mouth more than my daily bread."
JOB 23:12 NIV

Lord, I am always hungry. It seems I can't go too long without a
meal or a snack! May I be as hungry for Your Word as I am for
breakfast, lunch, and dinner. Your Word is greater than my daily
bread. Food can only nourish my body, but Your holy scriptures
sustain my spirit and my mind. May I stay focused on Your Word
and Your ways. Amen.

* * * * * * * *

"Heaven and earth will pass away, but my words will never pass away."
MATTHEW 24:35 NIV

Most things are temporary, God. I don't even have some of the
stuffed animals I had a few years ago. Books and special toys I
had as a little boy are long gone. We sell things in garage sales.
We throw things away. You tell us in Your Word that even the
earth will pass away. One thing that will never pass away is Your
Word. May I spend time reading and studying the Bible. It is very
important. It is eternal. Amen.

Therefore, we never stop thanking God that when you received his message from us, you didn't think of our words as mere human ideas. You accepted what we said as the very word of God—which, of course, it is. And this word continues to work in you who believe.

1 THESSALONIANS 2:13 NLT

God, Your Word is at work. It draws sinners to repent of sins. It draws hearts to trust in Jesus. Your Word is not just made up of human ideas; it came straight from You. That is what makes it stand out from all other books. Your Word has great power. Help me to tap into the power source of the Bible by committing to read it more regularly. Amen.

"Make them holy by your truth;
teach them your word, which is truth."
JOHN 17:17 NLT

Lord, it is good to know that the Bible is true. It is not a book
of fairy tales or fantasies. It is a book filled with stories of real
men and women. It tells me about Jesus—when he was born in
Bethlehem and all about His ministry on earth. It is a precious
book of truth. I love Your commands because they keep me safe
and they are best for me. I love Your Word, Father. Amen.

* * * * * * * * *

"My sheep listen to my voice; I know them,
and they follow me."
JOHN 10:27 NLT

Dear Lord, I like to think of You as my Good Shepherd. I know
Your voice. I am familiar with it because I read Your Word and
I have Your Holy Spirit living in me and counseling me in Your
ways. Like sheep who know their master's voice even among a
group of shepherds and can pick it out and follow after the right
one, I follow You. May I never turn my ear to another master. I love
You, my Shepherd, and I love Your Holy Word. Amen.

"So is my word that goes out from my mouth: It will not return to me empty, but will accomplish what I desire and achieve the purpose for which I sent it."
ISAIAH 55:11 NIV

Just as rain makes the grass, trees, and flowers grow, Your Word makes people grow. It is preached in churches and read by millions. It serves its purpose: many come to know You through its powerful message of Good News. You want us to read Your Word, learn from it, and live according to what it says. Your Word is powerful like a double-edged sword. May I be a listener and a learner and use Your Word wisely. May I take it seriously so that it may accomplish its purpose in my life. Amen.

I have taken your words to heart so I would not sin against you.
PSALM 119:11 NCV

God, hide Your Word in my heart so that I can take it with me wherever I go. Write Your ways on my heart that I might walk in them every single day. I do not want to sin against You. I want to remain pure, and I want to be kind and loving. I want to shine the light of Jesus into the world around me. Show me scriptures that will help me most so that I can memorize them and remember them when I need to. In Jesus' name I pray. Amen.

* * * * * * * * *

Everything that was written in the past was written to teach us.
The Scriptures give us patience and encouragement
so that we can have hope.
ROMANS 15:4 NCV

Dear God, Your Word has been around for a long, long time. People were encouraged by it and taught by it many years ago just as we are today. It has stood the test of time, and You declare that it is eternal. It will never pass away. May I become patient and find hope through the reading of Your Word. May I recognize the power of Your Word. In Jesus' name I pray. Amen.

> "The grass withers and the flowers fall,
> but the word of our God endures forever."
> ISAIAH 40:8 NIV

Dear God, I cherish the Bible and I ask You to help me be more serious about reading it daily. I know that it has the secret treasure that I long to find. It is not actually hidden but is available to me if I will only pray and ask Your Holy Spirit to reveal Your truths to me. I wonder why I put it off so much. I do other things like homework and messing around with electronics. I talk or text with my friends. Then it seems I am too tired to read the Bible. Help me to make time in the mornings to read Your Word and to pray. Help me to truly cherish Your Word. Amen.

MY DREAMS—
THE POWER OF EXPECTATION

Without dreams, there would be no hope. Perhaps you dream of being an engineer or a lawyer one day. Maybe your dream is to be a husband and father. Is there an instrument you would like to play in the high school band one day? Do you want to play a sport? Have you considered where God fits in with your dreams? We cannot see God, but faith is hope in that which we cannot see. We know God is there. We see Him in His wonderful creation all around us. We sense His closeness when we pray. God has promised that He has great plans for you. Pray for plans that match His will. If there is a dream that you have had for a long time, don't give up. Keep praying and asking God for whatever it is, but remember that He may have different plans for you. If so, they will be even better than your wildest imagination. He is a good God, and He loves to make dreams come true.

The love of money causes all kinds of trouble.
Some people want money so much that they have
given up their faith and caused themselves a lot of pain.
1 Timothy 6:10 cev

God, I sometimes count up all of my money and dream of what I will buy when I have more. I know that this is not a bad thing for a kid to do really, and yet I don't want to focus on money. I know that when I have money, it usually makes me want more. I spend a lot of time thinking of what I can buy with it. Help me never to put dreams of money above You in my life. I don't want to get caught up in material things. Amen.

**If you obey the Lord, you will be happy,
but there is no future for the wicked.**
PROVERBS 10:28 CEV

Heavenly Father, I want to have a good life. I want to walk in Your ways, and I want to be happy. I know that true happiness is found in You. As I make plans for my future and dream big dreams, please help me always to remember that life is only worth living if I am walking with You. I want what You want. I love You, Lord. Amen.

✳ ✳ ✳ ✳ ✳ ✳ ✳ ✳

Let all that I am wait quietly before God, for my hope is in him.
PSALM 62:5 NLT

God, I get in such a hurry. It seems that everything around me is moving fast. We all want what we want, and we want it now. Right now, in this moment, I rest in You. I sit quietly before You and I take time to remember where my hope comes from. It comes from the sovereign God of the universe who made the world and everything in it. You are my hope. I will wait before You. Amen.

"Ask me and I will tell you remarkable secrets
you do not know about things to come."
JEREMIAH 33:3 NLT

Lord, I think I have it all mapped out—what school I will go to, what I want to be, where I want to live. . . . But You know everything. You have amazing secrets that You will reveal to me as I am ready and as I listen to You. Help me to dream big but also to wait on You to reveal Your plans to me. I am safest when I follow You. Amen.

* * * * * * * * *

Whether you turn to the right or to the left, you will hear
a voice saying, "This is the road! Now follow it."
ISAIAH 30:21 CEV

It is of great comfort to me, God, that You are always with me. No matter where I go in life, You are with me pointing the way. You are revealing to me what I should do. If I follow a dream, You will be there guiding me. If I make a mistake or my heart gets broken along the way, You will still be there. Help me to know when to take a risk, when to step out in faith, when to follow my heart. Help me also to know when to make the safer and wiser choice. Amen.

> Much dreaming and many words are meaningless.
> Therefore fear God.
> ECCLESIASTES 5:7 NIV

God, help me not to daydream so much that I miss today. I catch myself drifting into a fantasy world where things are different or better, where I am happier or in a different set of circumstances. Keep me in the moment. Help me to trust You. I love You, God, and I respect You. I want only what You want for all of my days. Amen.

* * * * * * * *

> I say to myself, "The LORD is my portion;
> therefore I will wait for him."
> LAMENTATIONS 3:24 NIV

Dear God, I get so impatient sometimes. I want all of my dreams to come true now! And yet I look at Your creation and I am reminded of Your great power. You cause the sun to come up in the morning and to set in the evening. You are in control of my life because I have trusted in Jesus as my Savior. I choose today to wait patiently, asking You to allow my dreams to come true if they are in Your will for my life. Amen.

Do not be anxious about anything, but in every situation,
by prayer and petition, with thanksgiving,
present your requests to God.
PHILIPPIANS 4:6 NIV

God, I worry—I admit it. I worry about what people think of me. I worry about school. I worry about the future stretched out before me. It is overwhelming. When people ask me what I dream of being when I grow up, sometimes I think to myself that I am not sure I want to grow up! It is scary. Help me to trust You. I bring my worries about the future to You in prayer. I will live one day at a time as You unfold Your plans for my life. Amen.

> But now, Lord, what do I look for? My hope is in you.
> PSALM 39:7 NIV

Heavenly Father, I don't want to get so caught up in my hopes and dreams that I forget what is most important. I have all I could ever ask or hope for in my relationship with You. You are before all things, and through You all things were created and hold together. What more could I dream of than the ability to walk and talk with You, God? You are enough for me. Amen.

* * * * * * * * *

> For you have been my hope, Sovereign LORD,
> my confidence since my youth.
> PSALM 71:5 NIV

Lord Jesus, I am young still, but I have put my trust in You. I know that no matter what circumstances I am in now or where my dreams may lead me as a teenager and adult, You will be my hope. You are always with me. You never stop loving me no matter what. You make me strong and brave. You walk with me every step of the way. Please help me to remember that You are where I must place my hope and trust. Amen.

There is surely a future hope for you, and your hope will not be cut off.
PROVERBS 23:18 NIV

God, I long to grow up and be able to do anything I want, and yet I know Your timing is perfect. You knit me together in my mother's womb. You know the number of hairs on my head. The Bible tells me that You have a future for me and that because I am a believer who follows in Your ways, my hope will never be cut off. Help me to be patient and to know that all of my dreams cannot come true today. I have hope for a very bright future because of You. Amen.

* * * * * * * * *

With all your heart you must trust the LORD and not your own judgment. Always let him lead you, and he will clear the road for you to follow.
PROVERBS 3:5–6 CEV

God, You are trustworthy. You will never lead me astray. You know my heart and all the hopes and dreams it holds. Please help me to find the right paths and chase the right dreams in my life. I want to walk on the paths that will bring glory and honor to Your name. I want to walk on straight and narrow roads rather than following the crowd. I trust You, Father, to lead me in the right direction. Amen.

> **Your heart will be where your treasure is.**
> **LUKE 12:34 NCV**

Heavenly Father, it is hard not to dream of having things that I see others enjoying. I see games or electronics that my friends have, and I long to possess them also. I wish for the latest styles in clothing or the newest type of shoes the kids are wearing. May I pause in these moments to think of my true treasure. My true treasure is You. May I never dream of things that are of this world so much that I lose sight of my treasure. Amen.

* * * * * * * * *

> **When doubts filled my mind,**
> **your comfort gave me renewed hope and cheer.**
> **PSALM 94:19 NLT**

Heavenly Father, sometimes I get down and I cannot see beyond my sadness and disappointments. I forget about dreams and goals. I feel depressed. You are my Comforter. You are the only one who can bring back my sense of purpose and my happiness. You cheer me up and set me on the right path again, a path of hope and dreams and joy. I love You, Lord. You are so good to me. Amen.

"For I know the plans I have for you," declares the LORD,
"plans to prosper you and not to harm you,
plans to give you hope and a future."
JEREMIAH 29:11 NIV

Dear God, thank You that You already know my future. You tell me
in Your Word that You have good plans for me. Thinking about
the future is scary sometimes, but I will try to trust that You have
it all under control. I have dreams for my future, but I believe that
You know what is best for me. Please bring about Your will in my
life day by day as I walk with You. Please help my desires to match
Your will. Amen.

MY FAMILY—
THE POWER OF LOVE

Family. It is a powerful word. It makes us think of love and laughter, but it can also bring to mind thoughts of arguments and struggle. Sometimes we fight the most with those we love the most. Sometimes we take our family members for granted. Do you ever stop to think of all that your mom and dad do for you? Do you show love to those in your family, those God has given you as the closest people in your life? When we follow God's plan for loving our families and we shine for Him in the midst of even difficult situations, He will bless us. Family is important to God, and He has chosen your family for you. He knit you together in your mother's womb. He knows your name and the number of hairs on your head. He is involved in the details of your life. Whether you live with your birth parents, adoptive parents, one parent, or a guardian, He has chosen the authority figures in your life. He wants you to honor them. Take time to thank Him for the gift of family and remember that it is important to love your family well.

Children, obey your parents in the Lord, for this is right.
"Honor your father and mother"—which is the first commandment
with a promise—"so that it may go well with you
and that you may enjoy long life on the earth."
EPHESIANS 6:1–4 NIV

Heavenly Father, thank You for my parents and for their authority in my life. I want to go my own way, do my own thing, and find my own way in the world. But I know that they have been put over me to help me. I will obey them. Unless they direct me to do something that goes against Your Word, I will always choose obedience. Give me a heart of submission that honors the authority in my life. I know that You want this of me. Amen.

"Honor your father and your mother, so that you may live long in the land the LORD your God is giving you."
EXODUS 20:12 NIV

Dear God, sometimes I find it easy to obey my parents. Other times they seem so unreasonable and don't understand me at all. I get frustrated and angry. Please remind me in those moments that You have put my parents in a place of authority in my life and You want me to honor them. Give me the ability to hold my tongue. Help me to be calm and to show respect. Amen.

* * * * * * * *

Those who bring trouble on their families inherit only the wind. The fool will be a servant to the wise.
PROVERBS 11:29 NLT

Dear heavenly Father, You put me in my family. You decided exactly the family I should be in and You gave each member to me as a gift. No family is perfect, but I do love mine. We have good days and bad days, joys and sorrows, fun times and bad arguments. Help me to shine Your light into my family. Help me to bring them only good, never harm. May I forgive quickly and love strongly. Amen.

"As for me and my family, we will serve the LORD."
JOSHUA 24:15 NCV

Lord, I look around me and I see all kinds of people. I see all kinds of families making all kinds of choices about what is important. Some make sports their god. Others worship TV shows or travel. I want to serve You. I want You to be the most important part of my life, and I would love it if my whole family felt the same way. If we put You first in everything we do, I know that the rest will fall into place as it should. Amen.

* * * * * * * * *

My child, listen when your father corrects you.
Don't neglect your mother's instruction.
PROVERBS 1:8 NLT

God, I am getting a little older, and sometimes I just want to do things my way. It is hard always having to listen to my parents tell me what to do and when and how to do it. Give me a heart that tries to understand that they love me. Help me to realize that sometimes they really do know best. They have been living longer than me, and I know they have my best interest at heart. Help me to treat my parents as I should. Amen.

To discipline a child produces wisdom,
but a mother is disgraced by an undisciplined child.
PROVERBS 29:15 NLT

Lord, I get so upset when I am grounded or punished by my parents. I feel frustrated, and I don't like the feeling that I have disappointed them. I realize that one of the reasons You have put my parents in my life is to discipline me. Discipline is never fun, but I know You say in Your Word that it is necessary. Give me the grace to accept my parents' decisions, and help me to learn from my mistakes and from my consequences. Amen.

* * * * * * * * *

Therefore, whenever we have the opportunity, we should do good to everyone—especially to those in the family of faith.
GALATIANS 6:10 NLT

Lord, remind me that every believer in Christ is part of my family. They are my brothers and sisters through You. Put before me opportunities to show love to other Christians. Whether it is helping an elderly person or someone younger than me, give me a heart of love. Help me to see and grasp chances to brighten others' days and to help them in any way I can. I know this is important. Amen.

Love is patient and kind. Love is not jealous, it does not brag, and it is not proud. Love is not rude, is not selfish, and does not get upset with others. Love does not count up wrongs that have been done. Love takes no pleasure in evil but rejoices over the truth. Love patiently accepts all things. It always trusts, always hopes, and always endures.

1 CORINTHIANS 13:4—7 NCV

Lord, I love my family members. Some days it is easy. Other days it is not so easy. Some days I feel like loving them, and other days it takes all I've got just to be nice to them. At times I make bad choices. I am rude or selfish. I lash out with words that are not kind, words that I know do not please You. Help me to remember that You love me just as much when I am bad as when I am good. Help me to love my family every day, no matter what. Amen.

> God decided in advance to adopt us into his own family
> by bringing us to himself through Jesus Christ. This is what
> he wanted to do, and it gave him great pleasure.
> EPHESIANS 1:5 NLT

Dear God, thank You for bringing me into Your family through Jesus Christ. Thank You for choosing to adopt me as Your own child. You didn't have to do that. You wanted to. You wanted me as Your little sheep, Good Shepherd. You selected me. Thank You, God. It feels good to know the voice of my Shepherd will always direct my paths. It feels good to belong with You. You are my safety and my joy. I love You, Lord. Amen.

* * * * * * * * *

> "The second command is this: 'Love your neighbor as you love
> yourself.' There are no commands more important than these."
> MARK 12:31 NCV

God, love shows up again and again in the Bible. It must be important to You. It must be powerful. I know that it is. You tell me to love my neighbor as myself. When I stop to think about it, my neighbors are anyone I meet. They include my family, classmates, teachers, friends, and teammates. Help me this day to find little ways to show great love to those around me, especially those who live under the same roof with me! Amen.

Those who have been born into God's family do not make a practice of sinning, because God's life is in them. So they can't keep on sinning, because they are children of God.

1 JOHN 3:9 NLT

God, thank You for sending Jesus to die for my sins, making a way for me to be part of Your family. No earthly father is perfect, but You are my heavenly Father and You are above all things. Your ways are wise, and in Your perfection You make no mistakes. You have chosen my earthly family and planted me in it. Give me grace to love my family well. I am so blessed to be a child of the Living God, and I am also blessed to have a family where I belong and matter. Amen.

> You, your children, and your grandchildren must respect the LORD
> your God as long as you live. Obey all his rules and commands
> I give you so that you will live a long time.
> DEUTERONOMY 6:2 NCV

Dear heavenly Father, some people have a heritage of a family that loves and serves You. Others are the first in their families to follow Jesus. Either way, You promise blessing to those who follow You and who lead their families in Your ways. Help me to stand out as a believer and help my family to be blessed through my faithfulness to You. I want You always to be honored as the King of kings and Lord of lords in my family. Amen.

* * * * * * * * *

> Jacob was the father of Joseph. Joseph was the husband of Mary,
> and Mary was the mother of Jesus. Jesus is called the Christ.
> MATTHEW 1:16 NCV

Jesus, You had an earthly family. You grew up with a mom and dad and siblings. Even though God was Your Father, You worked with Your earthly father in his wood shop. You learned from him how to be a good carpenter. The Bible says Your mother was a woman who cherished things in her heart. She sounds like a loving person. Help me to honor my parents as You honored Yours. It is not always easy, Jesus. Amen.

She had a sister called Mary, who sat at the Lord's feet listening to what he said. But Martha was distracted by all the preparations that had to be made. She came to him and asked, "Lord, don't you care that my sister has left me to do the work by myself? Tell her to help me!" "Martha, Martha," the Lord answered, "you are worried and upset about many things, but few things are needed—or indeed only one. Mary has chosen what is better, and it will not be taken away from her."

LUKE 10:39–42 NIV

Jesus, I find myself not much different from Martha sometimes. I want to tell on my siblings for doing things I think they shouldn't be doing. I could learn a lot from Mary, the sister who sat at Your feet and listened to Your teachings. I am a busybody at times. Help me to slow down and listen for Your still, small voice. And help me to realize that my siblings may be different from me. You gave us all different personalities and gifts. Help me not to judge or boss them. Let me leave that to You! Amen.

MY FEARS—
THE POWER OF FAITH

Jesus came that we might be saved by grace through faith in His death on the cross for our sins. He rose again three days later and appeared to many. Then He ascended into heaven where He sits at God's right hand. He will come again to gather His followers. If you have placed your faith in Christ, you can look forward to eternal life. Actually, it has already begun in the abundant life available to you on earth. It all starts with faith. No one can make the decision to follow Jesus for you. It is a personal choice. It is believing in someone and something that you cannot see before you but that you trust in just the same. There is great power in faith. It will carry you through your darkest days, and it will encourage others as they wonder how you can face such trials without being shaken in your love for Jesus. Ask God to build up your faith. According to the Bible, there is great power even in faith the size of a tiny seed.

Jesus said to the woman,
"Your faith has saved you; go in peace."
LUKE 7:50 NIV

God, I read about Your miracles. Many times You mention the person's faith, so faith must be important to You. You tell us in Your Word that even if we have faith the size of a mustard seed, it is enough to move mountains. I want to have that kind of faith, Lord. Some days I don't think mine is even as big as that tiny seed. Give me faith that grows with each passing day. I love You, Lord. Amen.

* * * * * * * * *

So that your faith might not rest on human wisdom,
but on God's power.
1 CORINTHIANS 2:5 NIV

Lord, sometimes I try to figure it all out—my future, my worries. Then I usually come around to remembering that my faith must be in You, not in my own weak ways and abilities. I can't understand things or fix them, but You can. You are all-powerful and all-knowing, and You care about the circumstances of my life. I choose to place my faith in Your power and not my own today. Amen.

**Because of Christ and our faith in him,
we can now come boldly and confidently into God's presence**
EPHESIANS 3:12 NLT

I am not confident in and of myself, God. I find myself frightened when kids at school say mean things to me or call me names. I begin to believe them sometimes. I know that Jesus died for me. I truly do have faith. Help me to be bolder and more confident at school. Remind me that You are always with me and that through my faith in Christ, I have a mighty God at my side day in and day out. Amen.

* * * * * * * * *

Be on your guard; stand firm in the faith; be courageous; be strong.
1 CORINTHIANS 16:13 NIV

God, I find great strength in my faith. When others ask me why I won't do something that I know goes against Your Word, I lean on my faith. I am strong and bold in You because I trust You to back me up when I am in a corner. When I am tempted, I have the ability to stand firm against the devil's tricks. I lean on my faith. Thank You, Father, for helping me to have faith. Strengthen and grow my faith so that it is even greater, I ask. Amen.

In the same way, faith by itself,
if it is not accompanied by action, is dead.
JAMES 2:17 NIV

Lord, help me to stand out as different from nonbelievers who do not place their faith in You. May my actions and my words cause others to wonder why I do and say the things I do. May my good works point lost people to faith in You. Faith without works is dead. That is a strong statement. May my works glorify You and honor You. I want to live out my faith in my school, my neighborhood, and everywhere I go. In Jesus' name I pray. Amen.

* * * * * * * * *

I have been crucified with Christ and I no longer live,
but Christ lives in me. The life I now live in the body, I live by faith
in the Son of God, who loved me and gave himself for me.
GALATIANS 2:20 NIV

Jesus, living by faith is so freeing. I don't have to try to get everything right. And I am not just living for what makes me happy. The things that are important in this world are so unimportant in Your kingdom. Material wealth is nothing. Popularity is nothing. Give me the strength to resist the urge to look back at my sinful nature. It is always there, but You are stronger. Increase my faith, I pray. Amen.

> So in Christ Jesus you are all children of God through faith.
> GALATIANS 3:26 NIV

Heavenly Father, what a blessing it is to be called a child of the living God. It is not through anything I have done or will ever do that I am saved. I am saved by grace, through my faith in Jesus. It is Jesus who makes the way for me to come before You even now and know that You hear my prayers. Faith is the bridge that I can cross in order to stand before You. Thank You for faith in Christ that gives me eternal hope and joy. Amen.

* * * * * * * *

> When we get together, I want to encourage you in your faith,
> but I also want to be encouraged by yours.
> ROMANS 1:12 NLT

Make me an encourager, Lord. When I am with other believers, help me not to just soak up blessings but also to give. I am so encouraged when I hear others' stories. Make me aware that my own testimony is powerful as well. I want to encourage others to stand strong in their faith. Give me opportunities to do just that, and give me boldness to share what You are doing in my life that I might boast in Your glory! Amen.

The disciples went and woke him, saying, "Master, Master, we're going to drown!" He got up and rebuked the wind and the raging waters; the storm subsided, and all was calm. "Where is your faith?" he asked his disciples. In fear and amazement they asked one another, "Who is this? He commands even the winds and the water, and they obey him."
LUKE 8:24–25 NIV

Jesus, I almost want to laugh at the disciples—or scold them. It seems so crazy to me that they would fear drowning when You were aboard their boat! Didn't they know that You were God? The storms and the waves have nothing on the Master of the universe! But I would probably have been the same as they were, calling out to You in worry. I don't trust You with my circumstances sometimes. I get worried even though I know You are right here with me. Give me great faith, Lord. I want to trust You more. Amen.

**We are made right with God by placing our faith in Jesus Christ.
And this is true for everyone who believes, no matter who we are.**
ROMANS 3:22 NLT

Dear heavenly Father, sometimes I feel like I have messed up one too many times. I feel like I can't come to You again and apologize and ask You to "take me back." This is just a feeling. It is not truth. The truth is that I am not made right with You through my actions. I am made right with You through Jesus. Forgive my sins this day, Lord. And remind me that I can always come before You in faith. No matter what. Amen.

* * * * * * * * *

**But people are counted as righteous, not because of their work,
but because of their faith in God who forgives sinners.**
ROMANS 4:5 NLT

God, You are so faithful to me. You never waver the way I do. I am glad I serve a faithful God. I know that I am not counted righteous because of what I do. I know that righteousness comes only through the free gift of salvation. I do want to please You, though, Lord. I want to live out my faith. Thank You for showing Yourself faithful in my life on the good days and the bad alike. Make me faithful as well. I will never be perfect, but I can grow in my faith. Amen.

Because of our faith, Christ has brought us into this place of
undeserved privilege where we now stand, and we confidently
and joyfully look forward to sharing God's glory.
ROMANS 5:2 NLT

Jesus, I don't deserve the privilege of sharing in God's glory. It is undeserved—like a Christmas or birthday gift. Like a debt paid off by another who owed nothing but took on the great debt I owed. You have given me the free gift of salvation and forgiveness of my sins, abundant life now, and eternal life in heaven with You when I die. I humbly thank You for the gift. I place my faith in You this day and walk with You, my Savior. Amen.

* * * * * * * * *

He guards the paths of the just
and protects those who are faithful to him.
PROVERBS 2:8 NLT

God, Your protection is very apparent in my life. I feel it. I sense it. You lay out the way I should go, and if I am paying attention, I see it and follow in it. Help me always to remain faithful to You. When I stray, I sometimes wind up on a road that leads to nowhere. Protect my heart and mind, Lord, from the ways of the world. I want to faithfully follow You. In Jesus' name I pray. Amen.

> So we fix our eyes not on what is seen, but on what is unseen,
> since what is seen is temporary, but what is unseen is eternal.
> 2 CORINTHIANS 4:18 NIV

Lord, I like proof. I look for it. I like to hold things in my hand. I like to see how they work. Faith is not like that. It is not something I can see, but it is very real nonetheless. I look around me and realize that most of what I see is temporary. You are eternal. I will choose to fix my eyes on Jesus. In doing so, the world becomes dim in the light of His amazing grace. Amen.

* * * * * * * * *

> Now faith is confidence in what we hope for
> and assurance about what we do not see.
> HEBREWS 11:1 NIV

Dear God, sometimes I feel beaten down. There are bullies at school who act ugly. They can make people feel really bad about themselves. I am thankful that I have confidence through You that You are with me. I know that I matter to You and that You see me as Your precious child, not the way the bullies define me. I know that things will get better. I have to face my fears and trust that a brighter day is coming. I find a calm assurance in being Your child. Amen.

> But you, dear friends, by building yourselves up in your most holy faith and praying in the Holy Spirit, keep yourselves in God's love as you wait for the mercy of our Lord Jesus Christ to bring you to eternal life.
> JUDE 1:20–21 NIV

Dear Jesus, so many things tear me down in this world. My faith builds me up instead. When I spend time in Your Word and in prayer each day, I find great strength. I feel prepared to face the day no matter what is thrown at me. I am learning that faith requires waiting. I must wait on Your will and Your plans for my life to unfold. I must wait on Your second coming. It will be glorious. I love You, Lord. Amen.

* * * * * * * *

> Let love and faithfulness never leave you; bind them around your neck, write them on the tablet of your heart.
> PROVERBS 3:3 NIV

God, I love that my faith can go with me wherever I go. If I am at school, I can whisper a prayer to You as I walk down a hallway or begin to take a hard exam. If I am out with my friends, I can lean on my faith to help me face temptations—whether to gossip or to take part in other things I know displease You. May I be found faithful to You in every situation. In Jesus' name I pray. Amen.

MY FRIENDS— THE POWER OF CONNECTION

Friends are the family we get to pick! It is so important to choose Your friends carefully. God desires for His children to connect with other Christians. You need the support of others who view the world the way You do. Nonbelievers do not make decisions in the same way believers do. This is not to say that Christian friends are perfect or will never steer You in the wrong direction or let You down. But those who are truly following God will be more likely to be solid friends and give godly advice when You ask for it. There is great strength to be found in a true friend. It takes being a good friend to have a good friend, so ask God to make You a good friend to others and likewise to bless You with good friends.

Even my best friend, the one I trusted completely,
the one who shared my food, has turned against me.
PSALM 41:9 NLT

People mess up, Lord. They are only human. When a friend turns against me, it really hurts. Give me grace with those who hurt me. I know that I have hurt others, also. Forgive me for times when I have not been a true friend. God, I know that You are the only One who will never let me down. I choose to place my trust in You. Help me to be faithful to You. You are faithful to me no matter what. You are not like humans, God. Your friendship never fails. Amen.

"Why do you notice the little piece of dust in your friend's eye, but you don't notice the big piece of wood in your own eye?"
MATTHEW 7:3 NCV

God, I am so quick to judge my friends and to point out what they are doing wrong. When I look closely at my own life, I see just as many areas where I need to change and grow. Help me to be more tolerant of others' weaknesses. I should work to become a better friend myself rather than finding fault in others. Soften my heart and help me to see the good in my friends rather than the bad. In Jesus' name I pray. Amen.

* * * * * * * * *

While we were God's enemies, he made us his friends through the death of his Son. Surely, now that we are his friends, he will save us through his Son's life.
ROMANS 5:10 NCV

God, You are my truest Friend. You sought me out and saved me even though I was a sinner. I am truly saved by Your grace through Jesus, and I am very thankful for that. It is amazing to think that through Jesus' blood shed on the cross, my sins are forgiven and I can be a friend of the God of the universe. Thank You for being my very best Friend. You are always there. I love You, Lord. Amen.

Love prospers when a fault is forgiven,
but dwelling on it separates close friends.
PROVERBS 17:9 NLT

Heavenly Father, You are quick to forgive me, and yet sometimes I find it so hard to forgive others. Make me more forgiving. Remind me of my many sins and the great price You paid for them. You watched Your only Son die on a cross in order that my sins might be forgiven. I have no right to hold grudges or to be angry with others. Help me to be quick to forgive my friends when they wrong me. Amen.

* * * * * * * * *

There are "friends" who destroy each other, but a real
friend sticks closer than a brother.
PROVERBS 18:24 NLT

Give me a discernment, God, that can tell the difference between true friends and those who are not so true. There are all kinds of people in this world. Some people are only out for "number one." They will quickly turn on a friend. Give me loyal friends, I pray. I need friends who will be there through the good and the bad. I thank You for those few close friends in my life who stick closer than brothers or sisters. Amen.

*Wounds from a sincere friend are better
than many kisses from an enemy.*
PROVERBS 27:6 NLT

God, I have heard that it is good to speak the truth in love.
Sometimes when a friend tells me the truth, it hurts. It stings. I
think it is because I know they are right! Give me a heart that
accepts constructive criticism from friends. Give me wisdom to
know when I need to change based on what a friend shares with
me. It may not always be what I want to hear, but it is for my own
good. Amen.

* * * * * * * * *

As iron sharpens iron, so a friend sharpens a friend.
PROVERBS 27:17 NLT

Thank You, God, for Christian friends. Thank You for friends who
come alongside me and make me a better person. Thank You for
friends who encourage me to spend time in Your Word and to go
to church where I can be around other Christians. I need friends
like that. Please continue to provide Christian friends for me and
help me to be a good friend to others in my life. Amen.

"And if you are nice only to your friends, you are no better than other people. Even those who don't know God are nice to their friends."
MATTHEW 5:47 NCV

Heavenly Father, give me an opportunity today to be kind to someone who needs a smile or a word of encouragement. When I stick only in my little group of friends, I am not acting as Jesus did when He walked this earth. He noticed people around him who were sick or lonely. He spoke to them. I remember the story of Jesus going to Zacchaeus's home. Zacchaeus was someone who really needed a friend. Jesus changed His life by being that friend to him. Make me more like Jesus. Amen.

> Young people who obey the law are wise;
> those with wild friends bring shame to their parents.
> **PROVERBS 28:7** NLT

Dear God, I need Your help. I have not always been wise in picking my friends. Friends have a lot of power in my life. They can lead me in the right or the wrong direction. I want to have friends who are cool and popular, but sometimes those people are not the type of friends I need. They lead me down paths that are not pleasing to You to do things that my parents do not approve of. Give me discernment as I seek to choose friends who love and follow Your ways. Amen.

* * * * * * * * *

> The sweet smell of incense can make you feel good,
> but true friendship is better still.
> **PROVERBS 27:9** CEV

Heavenly Father, there is not much better than a good friend. I enjoy laughing and hanging out with my good friends. They lift my spirits. They make me forget my troubles and worries. Friends are a true blessing in my life. Thank You for providing good friends. I pray that I will always be a good friend to others. Help me to reach out to someone who needs a friend today. Amen.

> I am a friend to anyone who fears you—
> anyone who obeys your commandments.
> PSALM 119:63 NLT

Lord, it is amazing how I can visit another church—even one far from home—and feel comfortable. I find family there. Christ followers are my brothers and sisters. I have a lot in common with anyone who calls Jesus Lord and Savior. Even if we are different ages or from different backgrounds or cultures, we have the most important thing in common—You! Amen.

* * * * * * * * *

> A friend loves you all the time, and a brother helps in time of trouble.
> PROVERBS 17:17 NCV

God, I have a lot of friends who are just friends at school or friends on a sports team. They are fun to hang out with, but I would not share my deepest worries or struggles with them. Then there are those few friends You have put in my life that I can tell anything to. They are there when the sun is shining, but they also remain true when I am really down in the dumps. They "get it." They pray for me. They encourage me. They are solid and true friends. Thank You for the friends that love me all the time. In Jesus' name I pray. Amen.

> Jonathan had David reaffirm his oath out of love for him,
> because he loved him as he loved himself.
> **1 SAMUEL 20:17** NIV

Father God, David and Jonathan were friends who stuck closer than brothers. When I read about Jonathan loving David as himself, it challenges me. Do I love my friends in that way? Would I literally do anything for a friend? Am I quick to run when things get tough, or do I stick it out and remain true to my friends? I want to be a good friend. Show me the way to do this, I ask. Amen.

* * * * * * * * *

> The disciple Jesus loved was sitting next to Jesus at the table.
> **JOHN 13:23** NLT

Jesus, even You had "levels" of friends. You were a friend to all You met. You loved the world enough to die for all of us! But You had Your twelve closest friends, those who walked and talked with You—the ones we know as Your disciples. Even among the twelve, the Bible tells us there was "one You loved." It shows me that it is okay to have one friend who is closer than the rest. I pray that I will always have a close friend in my life. I pray that I will always be a best friend to someone as well. Amen.

A troublemaker plants seeds of strife;
gossip separates the best of friends.
PROVERBS 16:28 NLT

Gossip is tempting, God. I don't want to be one who spreads rumors or shares secrets only for the sake of stirring up problems. I pray that You will stop me just in time when I am about to share a juicy bit of news or something that is not necessary to tell others. Help me to be very careful of what I say. I know it is impossible to get the words back once they are spoken. You tell me in Your Word that the tongue can be used for good or for bad. Help me to build my friends up with my words and never tear them down. Amen.

MY FUTURE—
THE POWER OF PURSUING GOD'S PLAN

The future can seem overwhelming. It looms before you. You try to stretch your mind to imagine it, and yet you always fail. It is impossible for a human being to see the future. But what is impossible for man is possible for God. God is omniscient, all-knowing. He knows everything past, present, and future. He is in complete control of the universe. If you woke up this morning, He ordained it. This means He decided it would be good for you to live another day, take more breaths, and have more opportunities to shine as a light for Him in this world. Trust the Lord with the future; it is best left in His hands. He is big enough to handle your today and all of your tomorrows. Ask God each day to help you to trust Him and to follow Him. He will lead you into a bright future that He planned for you before you were born!

Does a fig tree produce olives, or a grapevine produce figs?
No, and you can't draw fresh water from a salty spring. If you are
wise and understand God's ways, prove it by living an honorable life,
doing good works with the humility that comes from wisdom.
JAMES 3:12–13 NLT

Dear God, I just want to honor You every day of my life. As people
look at me both today and in the future, please let them see the
light of Jesus in my life. No matter where You take me, no matter
what career I have or where I live, I want to do good works and
to love others. I want to be humble and to walk with You. I don't
know where I will be next year, much less when I am a grown-up.
But I want to keep walking with You. Amen.

"For I know the plans I have for you," declares the LORD,
"plans to prosper you and not to harm you,
plans to give you hope and a future."
JEREMIAH 29:11 NIV

The future seems really big, God. It hangs around out there in front of me, and yet I cannot see it or touch it. I can set goals and make plans, but I really have no idea what direction my life will take. I have to trust You. That is not easy for me. I like to be in control! As I face this day, give me the strength to surrender to Your plans for my life. Help me to enjoy this day and use it for Your glory, God. Help me to trust You with the days ahead. Amen.

* * * * * * * * *

What happens now has happened in the past, and what will happen in the future has happened before. God makes the same things happen again and again.
ECCLESIASTES 3:15 NCV

Heavenly Father, You are a God of order and patterns. You are consistent. You are constant, never changing. Just as You walked with Christ followers of past generations, You walk with us today. You will lead me just as You led those who came before me. You put Noah and his family on an ark to preserve their lives. You protected David from bears and even from a giant. I will trust that You will lead and protect me as well. Amen.

He is before all things, and in him all things hold together.
Colossians 1:17 niv

God, I have heard stories of crystal balls and fortune tellers. Certainly I don't approve of such things, and I stay away from them! I have to admit, though, that it would sometimes be nice to know where I am headed. The future is such a mystery, Father. Give me confidence to face life day by day, aware that I may not know the future but I know the One who holds it in his hands. In Jesus' name I pray. Amen.

* * * * * * * *

And we know that God causes everything to work together
for the good of those who love God and are called
according to his purpose for them.
Romans 8:28 nlt

Where will I go and what will I do in the future, Lord? It is hard to live day by day not knowing these things. I am afraid I will make a mistake. I am afraid I will mess up Your will and Your plan for my life. Scriptures can really comfort me when I begin to worry about this. You remind me with Your still, small voice that You are in control. You will use even my mess-ups for good. Amen.

God makes everything happen at the right time. Yet none of us
can ever fully understand all he has done, and he puts questions
in our minds about the past and the future.
ECCLESIASTES 3:11 CEV

Dear Lord, I have questions about the past and the future. I guess
it is just how we are put together as humans. We wonder about
what has been and about what is going to be. You are a good God.
You are sovereign. You make everything happen at the right time.
Even when I don't understand Your timing, it is perfect. I choose to
trust You and Your perfect timing in my life. Amen.

* * * * * * * *

"For my thoughts are not your thoughts, neither are your ways
my ways," declares the LORD. "As the heavens are higher than
the earth, so are my ways higher than your ways
and my thoughts than your thoughts."
ISAIAH 55:8—9 NIV

God, I have thoughts and plans, but You tell me in Your Word that
Your thoughts and Your plans are higher than mine. It is good to
know that someone wiser and bigger than me has great plans for
me. Help me to listen to Your still, small voice. Help me to walk in
Your ways and be guided by Your hand always. Even today. Amen.

In everything we have won more than a victory because of Christ who loves us. I am sure that nothing can separate us from God's love— not life or death, not angels or spirits, not the present or the future, and not powers above or powers below. Nothing in all creation can separate us from God's love for us in Christ Jesus our Lord!
ROMANS 8:37–39 CEV

Father, I feel afraid sometimes when I think about the future. I don't have any idea what will happen. I feel out of control. I find comfort in knowing that no matter what good or bad the future holds, You will never leave me. Your love is forever. You promise Your children that there is nothing that can separate us from Your love. Nothing. Not even the future with all of its unknowns. You will still be loving me in five years, ten years, and for all eternity. Wow! Amen.

The LORD knows all human plans; he knows that they are futile.
PSALM 94:11 NIV

Heavenly Father, I can worry and stress about the future, or I can realize that You have it all under control. You are the Creator. You keep the earth turning on its axis. You know each of Your children by name. You never sleep. You are always watching over us. My plans mean nothing compared to Yours. I know that You are good and that You have good plans for me. Thank You, Lord. Amen.

* * * * * * * *

The LORD will work out his plans for my life—for your faithful love,
O LORD, endures forever. Don't abandon me, for you made me.
PSALM 138:8 NLT

God, everyone is always asking me what I want to be when I grow up, and honestly, I have no clue. I mean, I have some ideas, but sometimes all the choices seem overwhelming. Help it to be enough that I am choosing to follow You with all my heart. You are faithful even when I stray away from You or begin to make my own plans and follow my own desires. You never leave me. I trust You to work out Your plans for my life. Amen.

They asked, "Who healed you? What happened?" He told them,
"The man they call Jesus made mud and spread it over my eyes
and told me, 'Go to the pool of Siloam and wash yourself.'
So I went and washed, and now I can see!"
JOHN 9:10–11 NLT

You can change my future in a moment, Lord. You are a difference
maker. You are a game changer. Just as You gave sight to the blind
and healed others of the horrible disease called leprosy, You can
change my current circumstances. Nothing is impossible with
You, God. Take the rough things in my life and change them if
You see fit. Use them to strengthen my character. Bring about the
future that You have planned for me, I pray. Amen.

* * * * * * * * *

Then the LORD said to Abraham, "Why did Sarah laugh? Why did she
say, 'I am too old to have a baby'? Is anything too hard for the Lord?
No! I will return to you at the right time a year from now,
and Sarah will have a son."
GENESIS 18:13–14 NCV

God, nothing is too hard for You. Nothing is impossible for a God
big enough to create the whole world! Even when things seem
impossible, they are not. You proved this when You allowed Sarah
and Abraham to have a baby in their old age. It seemed so crazy that
Sarah laughed when she heard the idea. But it happened. Help me to
believe in the impossible because I have a great big God. Amen.

> She is strong and is respected by the people.
> She looks forward to the future with joy.
> **PROVERBS 31:25 NCV**

Not having to fear the future is wonderful, Lord! I can choose faith over fear. I can choose resting in Jesus over running around worrying. I know that I will face hard times and bumps in the road along my journey, but I also know that as a Christian, I have nothing to fear. I can face the future with a smile on my face. You will never leave me or forsake me. Thank You, Lord. Amen.

* * * * * * * *

> You saw my body as it was formed. All the days planned for me
> were written in your book before I was one day old.
> **PSALM 139:16 NCV**

Creator God, You are really amazing. Before my mother even knew that I was growing in her belly, You knew. You decided the exact day that I would be born, and You have already planned out all of my days. Why would I worry about next week or next year? Why should I fear? I have the God of the universe watching over my steps. You are in control. Thank You for this comforting truth. In Jesus' name I pray. Amen.

"He said, 'The God of our ancestors chose you long ago to know his plan, to see the Righteous One, and to hear words from him. You will be his witness to all people, telling them about what you have seen and heard. Now, why wait any longer? Get up, be baptized, and wash your sins away, trusting in him to save you.' "
ACTS 22:14–16 NCV

You know what You are doing, don't You, God? You knew when Saul was a young boy growing up in a Jewish household that You would change the direction of his life. On a road to Damascus, on his way to kill Christians, You would shine a bright light and blind that man. You would change his plans! You made him into the greatest preacher of the Gospel who ever lived. Help me to be open to a direction change. I want to follow hard after You no matter where You lead me or how You choose to use me, Lord. Amen.

MY HABITS—
THE POWER OF GOOD CHOICES

Choices are the little life decisions *you* get to control. Like choosing to have chicken strips instead of a hamburger, or a fruit cup instead of fries. Some good choices have a happy ending, like a trip to the park or mall for being dependable with schoolwork, while other bad choices, like showing disrespect to your mom or dad, may mean temporarily losing something you like.

Imagine having two banks and a lot of pennies. One bank is only to be used when making good choices. The other bank is used for bad choices. If you put "habit pennies" in your banks for a month, how many do you think you'd have in each bank?

We become more like the choices we make. The more good choices you make the more good habits you'll have. The more bad choices you make the more bad habits will come between you and your family, teachers, and God.

The older you get the more choices you'll get to make. If you learn the power of good choices now, you can build good habits that keep up relationships in the future. What's your *choice*?

"The temptations in your life are no different from what others experience. And God is faithful. He will not allow the temptation to be more than you can stand. When you are tempted, he will show you a way out so that you can endure."
1 CORINTHIANS 10:13 NLT

Dear God, temptations are those times when I wrongly think that bad choices are good decisions. Many bad choices seem like a lot of fun. Some seem harmless. Sometimes friends want me to do what they do. When I know the right thing to do—help me to do it. I know You will help me get through temptations, and You expect me to talk to You about them as they come up, which is pretty often. It seems like it's always easier to do the wrong thing, and I don't want to. I will always need Your help. Amen.

Imitate God, therefore, in everything you do,
because you are his dear children.
EPHESIANS 5:1 NLT

Dear God, You always make the best choices. You made a way for me to be Your friend. I don't always make good choices. I also have some bad habits. Help me pay attention to the things You do so I can do them, too. If I can be more like You, then I can learn good habits. I want my choices to make You happy. I want my habits to be noticed for how they seem like something You would do. Amen.

* * * * * * * * *

Jesus replied, "I tell you the truth,
everyone who sins is a slave of sin."
JOHN 8:34 NLT

Dear God, Sometimes I just don't get it. I make a bad choice and right away I am upset with myself. Some people call the feeling You get when You sin a guilty conscience, and others call it the conviction of the Holy Spirit. All I know is I usually wish I hadn't done whatever it was I did. Sometimes I feel like I can't even stop myself from making a bad choice. Help me start making good choices because I don't want the bad choices to make me something I am ashamed of. Amen.

For the wages of sin is death, but the free gift of God is eternal life
through Christ Jesus our Lord.
ROMANS 6:23 NLT

Dear God, You sent Jesus to pay the price for my bad choices. You
call them sins. You also said if I were paid for making bad choices,
the payment would be death. That's a payment I don't want. I know
You want me to make good choices, and I am thankful You offer
eternal life when I make one really good choice—accepting the gift
of Jesus. After that choice help me continue to make good choices.
I know that's what You want, so help me want it, too. Amen.

* * * * * * * * *

Trust in the LORD with all your heart;
do not depend on your own understanding.
PROVERBS 3:5 NLT

Dear God, You said lying is a bad choice. Because You said it, I
know it's true, but I hear people lie all the time, and it doesn't seem
like anything bad happens to them. I see kids cheat in school and
get away with it. I've even seen people get hurt and no one seems
to care. Are there really kids who follow You? Maybe I don't have
to understand everything to know You want me to be truthful,
honest, and kind. Because You know more than me, help me trust
You to be right in everything. Amen.

Seek his will in all you do, and he will show you which path to take.
PROVERBS 3:6 NLT

Dear God, You want me to follow You without ever hearing Your voice. Talking to people is a lot easier than trying to guess what they're thinking. Since I can't talk to You face-to-face, help me to want to pray and then to read the Bible. You wrote some pretty amazing things for me to learn. Maybe someday I can talk to You like I do with my friends, but until then help me to learn what You've said so I can do what You ask. Amen.

* * * * * * * * *

You must remain faithful to the things you have been taught.
You know they are true, for you know you can
trust those who taught you.
2 TIMOTHY 3:14 NLT

Dear God, there are people in my church who help me learn more about You. I have to be honest: there are times when I don't pay as much attention as I should, but there are other times when what I learn is something new that can help me make good choices and better habits. You want me to do certain things, and I want to do what You want. I'm pretty certain I can't do it without You. Amen

Let's not get tired of doing what is good. At just the right time we will reap a harvest of blessing if we don't give up.
GALATIANS 6:9 NLT

Dear God, sometimes I make good choices because I want other people to notice. It's nice when they tell me I'm doing a good job. But that can't be the only reason to make good choices. Maybe I'm supposed to make good choices because You asked—even when no one notices, and even when I don't think there is any benefit. Doing the right thing is hard work, and sometimes there's no one to remind me to pay attention to the choices I make. Wait, You're always there. Help me remember. Amen.

> Just as you accepted Christ Jesus as your Lord,
> you must continue to follow him.
> COLOSSIANS 2:6 NLT

Dear God, You want people to come to You just as they are, but I'm also learning that You don't want them to stay like they were. If You didn't want them to change, then why would they need to be saved? I don't want to just say I love You and then act like You don't matter. That just doesn't make sense. I want my best choices to be the same choices You would make. Help me do that. Amen.

* * * * * * * * *

> Remain in fellowship with Christ so that when he returns, you will be
> full of courage and not shrink back from him in shame.
> 1 JOHN 2:28 NLT

Dear God, what would it be like if You came for a visit? You might ask me hard questions about the choices I'm making, the things I do when I'm with my friends, and the things I think about when I'm all by myself. What would I say? I don't want to make bad choices thinking You might not be looking. You aren't just my Friend; You're the One who saved me. Help me honor You in every choice I make. Amen.

Whatever you do or say, do it as a representative of the Lord Jesus, giving thanks through him to God the Father.
COLOSSIANS 3:17 NLT

Dear God, when people hear me say I am a Christian, I wonder what they think. Do they expect me to be different? Would they be surprised to notice more good choices than bad? I want to be like You. I want others to see that You make a difference in people who follow You. When I make bad choices, it makes You sad, and it makes other people think I'm not following You very well. Help me remember the main job of a follower is to follow. Amen.

Wise choices will watch over you.
PROVERBS 2:11 NLT

Dear God, I'm not sure why I didn't think of this before, but the people I trust most are people who make good choices. It can be fun hanging out with people who make bad choices, but I usually get in trouble, and I'm never sure they can be trusted. It seems like good choices make it possible for my mom and dad to trust me. When I do the right thing, we don't argue as much. When I do the right thing, I believe You're happy. Help me trust You to help me make good choices. Amen.

* * * * * * * *

I can do everything through Christ, who gives me strength.
PHILIPPIANS 4:13 NLT

Dear God, I keep hearing that some people don't think someone my age can make good choices. Some people just seem to want to try to help kids after they've made bad choices. I know I'm not an adult yet, but I think making good choices would be better than going through the trouble that always seems to come with bad decisions. You promised to help me, and I believe You can make me strong enough to say no to what I shouldn't do and yes to the things You want me to do. Thanks for Your help. Amen.

**A wise child accepts a parent's discipline;
a mocker refuses to listen to correction.**
PROVERBS 13:1 NLT

Dear God, there are times when I'm not sure my parents really understand what's it like to be me. They tell me to do things or not to do things, and I can't seem to figure out why it's so important. I know they are supposed to help me learn, so help me pay attention and be patient while I wait to really understand why what they say is so valuable. You want me to listen to my parents, so I need You to help me really listen and then obey. Amen.

MY HEART—
THE POWER OF HUMILITY

When you don't know who you are, you can either become prideful or think you aren't worth much.

As a Christian, you're a child of God. You're created for a purpose. You're given skills God can use. You have a capacity to love others, share adventures, be courageous, and do big things for a great God. If you think that makes you special, it does.

Jesus was God's only Son. He was with God from the beginning, and He always made right choices. There's no one like Him. If you think that makes Him special, it does.

However, Jesus humbled Himself and came to earth as someone like us. His greatest adventure was to die on a cross, rejected by those He loved and abused by those who should have protected Him. It was humility that allowed Jesus to become our Savior.

We may be children of God, but we should always be humble enough to serve, weak enough to accept God's strength, and trusting enough to accept God's great gifts. We serve faithfully, and if anyone applauds, we make sure God gets the credit.

If you think that makes God special, it does.

I know how to live on almost nothing or with everything.
I have learned the secret of living in every situation, whether it is
with a full stomach or empty, with plenty or little.
PHILIPPIANS 4:12 NLT

Dear God, Your words say that I don't have to have a lot of stuff
to be satisfied. Paul, one who served You, learned to live with
whatever You gave him. Maybe the secret is that no matter how
much or how little I have, You're still God, I'm still Your child, and
in the end I get to spend forever with You. Why should it matter
what I wear, how much I own, or where I live? You don't seem to
think those things matter. Help me be humble enough to accept
whatever You provide. Amen.

Pride leads to disgrace, but with humility comes wisdom.
PROVERBS 11:2 NLT

Dear God, You want me to know that when I show off, my actions look ugly to others. You don't want me to compare the size of my house, how much money I have, or the things I own with the things others have. Even if I think I know more than others, help me never praise myself. If others want to tell me about what they've accomplished, I should never allow their words to influence me to do the same thing. Your words say that when I'm humble I'm also wise. Help keep me from making accomplishments more important than people. Amen.

* * * * * * * * *

If I must boast, I would rather boast
about the things that show how weak I am.
2 CORINTHIANS 11:30 NLT

Dear God, You want me to boast but only about the things that show I can't do everything. As strange as that sounds, when I tell people about my struggles, it gives me an opportunity to share how awesome and helpful You are. I always thought being the best at everything was what I was supposed to be. Not everybody can be the best, but You can. Talking about You reminds me that the God who is above all calls me His child, and He has always been willing to teach me. Help me boast about my Teacher. Amen.

91

Haughtiness goes before destruction; humility precedes honor.
PROVERBS 18:12 NLT

Dear God, Your words say that pride always leads to ruin. When someone believes he is better, greater, bigger, and more important that anyone else, he may be ruined, because no one will want to listen to him brag. When I quietly do my work to the best of my ability and I work for You, then other people may decide to honor me, but I won't need to point out my greatest achievements. I don't have to be the greatest to know that serving You is the greatest honor I could ever have. Amen.

* * * * * * * * *

Fools think their own way is right, but the wise listen to others.
PROVERBS 12:15 NLT

Dear God, You don't want me to act like a know-it-all. When I refuse to listen to others and insist that my way is the only way, Your words say I'm being thoughtless. Help me allow others to share their ideas first. I may think I have the best way, but there are no teams that can be successful if only one person plays the game. You say I'm wise if I will take the time to really listen to others. Help me listen and then share my ideas when others want to know what I think. Amen.

All of you should be of one mind. Sympathize with each other.
Love each other as brothers and sisters. Be tenderhearted,
and keep a humble attitude.
1 PETER 3:8 NLT

Dear God, You're pleased when there is a room full of people who understand what it looks like to be humble. These people care about each other, share honest struggles, are compassionate, and decide that working together can serve You well. No one tries to prove he or she is better than anyone else, and no one feels unaccepted. This probably doesn't happen as much as You want it to, but it is what You ask. Help me work with other Christians to make it safe to serve You—together. Amen.

* * * * * * * * *

It is not that we think we are qualified to do anything on our own.
Our qualification comes from God.
2 CORINTHIANS 3:5 NLT

Dear God, You want to make me skilled to serve You. I don't start out that way, but when You ask me to serve, then You help me with the skills and equipment so it becomes possible to do things I never thought I could. You don't want me to brag that I already knew how to do the work. Without You I would fail to serve as well as when I let You help me learn new skills. If You make me qualified, I can serve. Help me qualify for Your service. Amen.

This is what the LORD says: "Don't let the wise boast in their wisdom, or the powerful boast in their power, or the rich boast in their riches."
JEREMIAH 9:23 NLT

Dear God, You don't like it when Your children boast about what they've done. A person can be wise without saying, "Hey, I'm pretty smart." A person who is well respected should not try to get others to do what he wants just because people like him. A person who has money shouldn't make others feel less important if they don't have as much. Your words say that it's hard to find friends when everything is all about me. Pride never says anything others like to hear. Help me choose humility. Amen.

> Let us not become conceited, or provoke one another,
> or be jealous of one another.
> **GALATIANS 5:26** NLT

Dear God, You don't want me to be a drama king. When I make sure others know my good points and that they don't measure up, or when I get upset because I think someone may be better than me, then I'm not following You. I'm using You to try to prove that I'm special. I can become so good at creating drama that my actions are filled with pride. When I am humble, I think of others first. When I follow You, I'm not promoting me. When You approve of my service, there's no need to be jealous. Amen.

* * * * * * * * *

> Live in harmony with each other. Don't be too proud to enjoy
> the company of ordinary people. And don't think you know it all!
> **ROMANS 12:16** NLT

Dear God, You tell me I'm both Your child and an ordinary guy. I'm in a special place because You love, forgive, and welcome me into Your family. I'm in a place of humility because the only thing that makes me different is that I believed in what Jesus did for me by taking on the payment for my sin. I shouldn't look at other people as less important. If You can rescue me, then You can rescue anyone. Help me to remember that Your grace and mercy rescue ordinary people and make them part of Your family. Amen.

He leads the humble in doing right, teaching them his way.
PSALM 25:9 NLT

Dear God, You want me to follow You and be prepared to learn. I don't think teachers like it when I act like there's nothing they can teach that I don't already know or act as if the information isn't important. I may think I'm being funny, but this type of response doesn't prove that I've made the choice to humbly follow You. If I treat other people in authority this way, then I am probably treating You that way, too. Teach me to make good choices, listen as You lead, and learn from Your words. Amen.

* * * * * * * * *

**Though the LORD is great, he cares for the humble,
but he keeps his distance from the proud.**
PSALM 138:6 NLT

Dear God, when I'm prideful You don't like being around me. You never leave, but You're sad to see me act as if I'm the most important person in the room. Your words say that You will always stay closer to people who are humble. When I'm humble, I understand that I'm weak and You offer the help I need to do the big things You ask. The moment I think I can do anything without You is the moment You let me try. You stand back and sadly watch me fail. Help me always choose the closeness of humility. Amen.

(Jesus said,) "Let me teach you, because I am humble and gentle
at heart, and you will find rest for your souls."
MATTHEW 11:29 NLT

Dear God, You want me to learn humility from You. Humility is
an attitude in serving that pleases You. Because I want to learn
humility, help me learn from the humblest man who ever lived.
Your Son, Jesus, was born in a stable, lived in a town most people
despised, and once said He didn't even have a pillow. Jesus
wants to teach me, and if I learn His lessons well, I will be totally
satisfied in following Him. Your Son shows me how to be humble.
Make me wise enough to follow His example. Amen.

* * * * * * * * *

Always be humble and gentle. Be patient with each other.
EPHESIANS 4:2 NLT

Dear God, it's easy to be proud, rough, and annoying, but You
want me to grow into someone who is humble, kind, and patient. I
couldn't run a race in school if I didn't show good sportsmanship,
practice in a way that shows I'm learning to endure, and care for
my team. It's painless to do what's easy, but You want me to do
what's right. I like to do things that entertain me, but You want me
to do things that bring joy. Help me learn humility that shows You
honor and brings me close to You. Amen.

Humble yourselves under the mighty power of God,
and at the right time he will lift you up in honor.
1 PETER 5:6 NLT

Dear God, You want me to understand that You're God and I'm
not. I'm Your child, but You know what needs to be done and how
to do it. When I do a good job, it's because I follow Your directions.
Help me give You the credit, because when I take the praise, I steal
Your honor. When I give You the credit, there will be a time when
You honor me for being faithful. I'd rather be a faithful child of
God than seek a spotlight meant for You. Help me always point
others to Your light. Amen.

MY IDENTITY—
THE POWER OF WHO I AM IN CHRIST

Have you ever thought about *what* you are? Sure, you have a name, and that helps everyone relate to you, but you're more than a name. You're someone's child, grandchild, cousin, student, friend, neighbor, study partner, guest, singer, athlete, gamer, or babysitter.

As a Christian you're something more than that. *Who* you are is a child of God. He loves you and has a plan for you to bring honor to the family name.

It's easy to forget who God says you are and live like there's no real difference between who you are and those who don't follow Jesus. Did you know that God says there should be a big difference? Did you know that He wants You to be different?

It can be hard to follow God when we don't know who God says we are. He described us as people who make a difference, people wise enough to know there's more to life than the tough things we face today, people who are compassionate enough to understand that people need to know about the God who makes us different.

Since you have been raised to new life with Christ,
set your sights on the realities of heaven, where Christ sits
in the place of honor at God's right hand.
COLOSSIANS 3:1 NLT

Dear God, You have the best future planned for me. I really don't
know what heaven is going to be like, but if You planned it,
then it's got to be pretty special. After all, You made Alaska, the
clownfish, and redwood trees. Every time I go to the zoo, I think
about how creative You are. Each animal is so different, and yet
You thought of what each one would be like. The God who made a
lemur can be trusted with knowing the best way to create heaven.
Right now? I'm thinking about being where You are. Amen.

Anyone who belongs to Christ has become a new person.
The old life is gone; a new life has begun!
2 CORINTHIANS 5:17 NLT

Dear God, You made me new. When I accepted Jesus as my Savior, You changed me. That must mean I am supposed to be different. If there isn't a difference in my life, maybe I'm not doing things right. You want me to understand things from a new point of view. Being kind, gentle, and loving is part of my new attitude. Help me practice what I know to be true about what the "new me" should be like. Help me stay away from the things that remind me of what I used to be. Amen.

* * * * * * * * *

My old self has been crucified with Christ. It is no longer I who live, but Christ lives in me. So I live in this earthly body by trusting in the Son of God, who loved me and gave himself for me.
GALATIANS 2:20 NLT

Dear God, You want me to trust You. The Bible says You will help me make right choices, and I *want* to live for You. The Bible says my old life died, and I only want to remember what it's like to really live the adventure You have for me now. It's easy to think about the way things used to be, so help me follow Your instructions. I believe You have something for me to do, so I will trust You to show me what that is, where I should go, and how I can serve You well. Amen.

> To all who believed him and accepted him,
> he gave the right to become children of God.
> JOHN 1:12 NLT

Dear God, You made me Your child. I believed in Jesus and accepted His forgiveness and life. That's when You called me Your child. I know what it's like to be a child, but You're God. You made this world. You told the stars where to stop in the night sky. You made oceans, mountains, volcanoes, and the Grand Canyon. You made animals, fish, and sunshine. You made me—and then called me Your child. You took my old life and gave me something new. You are so awesome. Thanks, Dad. Amen.

* * * * * * * * *

> Put on your new nature, created to be like God—
> truly righteous and holy.
> EPHESIANS 4:24 NLT

Dear God, You gave me an example to follow. I know I haven't arrived yet, but I want to press on. I can't become like you on my own, and I need Your help. My new life is amazing, but when I make mistakes, I try to fix them on my own, run from them, or decide I just can't go on. Help me to keep coming back to You when I sin. You are willing to forgive me. Help me be willing to talk to You—especially about the hard stuff. Thanks for always listening. Amen.

(Jesus said,) "I no longer call you slaves, because a master
doesn't confide in his slaves. Now you are my friends,
since I have told you everything the Father told me."
JOHN 15:15 NLT

Dear God, You're my Friend. You chose to be my best Friend, so
I want to do the same. I want our friendship to be close enough
that I can tell You anything. Help me to read the Bible. All Your
best advice is in there. It's pretty amazing to know that the God
who made everything wants to be my Friend. Making friends
can be hard, which makes it especially cool that You've always
wanted to be my Friend. I don't know why You keep amazing me,
but You do. Amen.

* * * * * * * * *

God saved you by his grace when you believed.
And you can't take credit for this; it is a gift from God.
EPHESIANS 2:8 NLT

Dear God, You gave the gift of grace. Sin is something that's easy
to do but hard to stop. It makes me feel bad, and I'm never sure
how to make up for it. When I believed in Jesus, You gave me
something I didn't deserve and could never earn—forgiveness and
love. Because all I have to do is accept Your gifts, I am thankful.
You didn't have to offer the gifts, but when I accept them, I am
closer to You, and I want to stay close. Help me always to come
back to You, right where I should be. Amen.

> I am certain that God, who began the good work within you,
> will continue his work until it is finally finished
> on the day when Christ Jesus returns.
> **PHILIPPIANS 1:6 NLT**

Dear God, some days I want to give up on me, but You never do. I am in the middle of a makeover, and I can't wait to see what You come up with. When I get my haircut, the barber asks me to move my head one direction or another. He knows how to give me a haircut, but I need to cooperate. That's just like You. As You work to change me, help me to cooperate. You see my potential. You know the possibilities. You never give up on me. That's awesome. Amen.

We are citizens of heaven, where the Lord Jesus Christ lives.
And we are eagerly waiting for him to return as our Savior.
PHILIPPIANS 3:20 NLT

Dear God, You're waiting for me to come home. I live here now, but someday You want me to be with You in heaven. The Bible tells me heaven is where I really belong. Jesus lives in heaven, and He promises to come back someday. That will be pretty wonderful. I wouldn't even trade it for a day off school, a vacation, or a birthday party. I'm getting to know You more every day, but I can't wait to meet You in person. Help me get ready. Amen.

* * * * * * * * *

God knew his people in advance, and he chose them to become
like his Son, so that his Son would be the firstborn
among many brothers and sisters.
ROMANS 8:29 NLT

Dear God, You understand me. You made me, love me, and have things You want me to do. Before I was even born, You knew me. Before I could say my first word, You wanted me to be a part of Your family. When I believed in Jesus, You made that possible. I've met some of Your family, but You have family all over the world, and I can't wait to meet everyone. No matter what anyone else thinks of me, I'm glad You understand and chose to love me. Amen.

Since God chose you to be the holy people he loves,
you must clothe yourselves with tenderhearted mercy,
kindness, humility, gentleness, and patience.
COLOSSIANS 3:12 NLT

Dear God, You're my Teacher. When someone gets in trouble, it's easy for me to think they deserve it, but when You offer forgiveness, I begin to think You look at things differently. When it would be easy to be rude, You want me to be kind. When I want to point out the things I'm good at, You want me to be humble. When I might want to answer roughly, You ask me to be gentle. When people seem slow, You want me to be patient. I have a lot to learn. Thanks for being a great teacher. Amen.

* * * * * * * * *

Stop telling lies. Let us tell our neighbors the truth,
for we are all parts of the same body.
EPHESIANS 4:25 NLT

Dear God, You want me to tell the truth. You know, it's easy for humans to lie. We do it a lot. But You want me to be a truth teller. Sometimes I get in trouble because when I tell the truth, I am also being honest about something I did wrong. Even then You want me to be honest. Maybe You do that so I don't have to live with secrets that make me unhappy. When I'm honest I can begin a better friendship with You and give others the chance to forgive me. Help me always to be truthful. Amen.

(Jesus said,) "I have loved you even as the Father
has loved me. Remain in my love."
JOHN 15:9 NLT

Dear God, You really love me. The Bible tells me Jesus loves me just like God loves Jesus. That's a lot of love. It's easy to understand why God loves Jesus—He's perfect. But I'm not perfect. I make mistakes. Jesus came to show His love by paying for my sin by dying on a cross. Now that's love. Jesus rose from the dead and made it possible for me to be with Him in heaven someday. Now that's a gift. God said He would meet all my needs. Now that's amazing. Thanks, God. Amen.

* * * * * * * *

We are Christ's ambassadors; God is making his appeal through us.
We speak for Christ when we plead, "Come back to God!"
2 CORINTHIANS 5:20 NLT

Dear God, You gave me good news to share. When I get a good grade on my report card, I want people to know. When I finish reading a book that seems hard, I want to celebrate. The words You put in the Bible are good news. Help me to read them, ask questions about what I don't understand, and then share with excitement the news that You offer forgiveness and love to everybody, even those I don't think would be interested. Help me to be Your ambassador. Amen.

Such things were written in the Scriptures long ago to teach us.
And the Scriptures give us hope and encouragement
as we wait patiently for God's promises to be fulfilled.
ROMANS 15:4 NLT

Dear God, Your promises are on the way. Because You're God, You keep every promise You make. Sometimes it seems like it can take a long time for some promises to come true, but when You promised Noah You would never again send a flood that covered the whole earth, You kept Your promise. When You said the Messiah (Jesus) would come, You kept that promise, too. You said we should be encouraged because You will keep even more promises. I believe You will do what You said You would do. Amen.

MY PURITY—
THE POWER OF THOUGHTS

Your imagination is a wonderful and powerful part of how God designed you. With your imagination, you can think of amazing places and fantastic adventures. With that same imagination, you can think about other things that never fit with God's plan for you.

Your mind is a place where good and bad ideas can grow side by side. All sin starts in your mind. You begin by thinking about things that shouldn't spend time in your brain. Thinking leads to imagining what it would be like to do something you know is wrong. The next step is letting your thoughts lead to actions that God warned against.

God wants your mind, heart, and body to be pure. He wants to rescue you from the pain of past sin, invite you to follow Him right now, and protect you for the future.

When you choose to concentrate on things that help you live like God asks, there is less room for thoughts that send out invitations to your own destruction.

What you allow inside your mind can either pull you closer to God or push you away from His embrace. Purity always pursues God.

Let God transform you into a new person by changing the way you think. Then you will learn to know God's will for you, which is good and pleasing and perfect.
ROMANS 12:2 NLT

Dear God, You want to change me, and You want to start with the way I think. Because I'm newly created by You, I should be willing to let You teach me a better way to think. Your words say You think differently than I do. Since You are God, I want to learn how to nourish pure thoughts. I can't know Your good, pleasing, and perfect choices for me if I don't allow room for Your thoughts to help me make right decisions. Help me purify my mind by making room for Your instructions. Amen.

Instead, clothe yourself with the presence of the Lord Jesus Christ. And don't let yourself think about ways to indulge your evil desires.
ROMANS 13:14 NLT

Dear God, You want me to accept Your presence like a favorite jacket. You bring comfort and remind me of Your constant help, and You're my best Friend. Sometimes I forget how close You are, and I get distracted thinking about things that You and I can't do together. I wish I didn't have these thoughts, but that's why I need You near me. I need You to remind me that the way I think should always tell me how much I need You. Purify my life, and may the thoughts in my mind bring You honor. Amen.

* * * * * * * *

Create in me a clean heart, O God. Renew a loyal spirit within me.
PSALM 51:10 NLT

Dear God, You want me to ask for a clean heart, but when I ask, it means You will need to make changes in me. If I have a clean heart, there are some jokes I shouldn't listen to or tell. When I let You clean the part of me that's connected to You, I will need to be careful what I watch, listen to, and think about. When You purify me, I need to ask You to take my decision to be loyal to You and make it a new choice every day. So, I'm asking. Amen.

Fix your thoughts on what is true, and honorable, and right, and pure, and lovely, and admirable. Think about things that are excellent and worthy of praise.
PHILIPPIANS 4:8 NLT

Dear God, You have a way for me to train my mind to connect with purity. Whenever I have a new thought, I need to ask a few questions. Is this thought true, honorable, right, pure, lovely, admirable, excellent, or worthy of praise? If the answer is no to any of these, then it's time to let the thought go and refuse to invite it back—it's not a good guest. If the thought matches the list, then it's a thought to pay attention to. Give me the wisdom to know when to send a thought away. Amen.

* * * * * * * * *

We prove ourselves by our purity, our understanding, our patience, our kindness, by the Holy Spirit within us, and by our sincere love.
2 CORINTHIANS 6:6 NLT

Dear God, You gave me six ways to show proof that You're changing me. My mind should show proof by being pure. My decisions should show understanding, patience, kindness, and love. My heart should be a home to Your Holy Spirit where He can guide me in the way You want me to go. May my commitment to You be useful in showing others You can change people from sinners to forgiven followers. Help me always remember that I serve You. I should do what You ask, avoid what makes me stumble, and show that You really do change lives. Amen.

Teach me your ways, O LORD, that I may live according to your truth!
Grant me purity of heart, so that I may honor you.
PSALM 86:11 NLT

Dear God, You want me to be a student of godly living and to honor You through a purity of heart that only You can give. If I just learn *facts* about Your truth, then I haven't learned enough. Help me take all the things You teach me and make the choice to live in a way that looks like what I'm learning, even when Your truth is different than my actions. When it comes to who's truth is really true, You are the winner every time. Teach me and let me live Your truth. Amen.

* * * * * * * *

God's truth stands firm like a foundation stone with this inscription:
"The LORD knows those who are his," and "All who belong
to the LORD must turn away from evil."
2 TIMOTHY 2:19 NLT

Dear God, You say that the best way for others to see You is for me to turn away from evil. Your truth should bring purity to my life when I choose to turn my back on everything that You say is off limits. If I don't, then I'm not following You very well. I'm so thankful that You forgive when I make a wrong choice, but I also want to make better choices today than I did yesterday. I want my heart, mind, and life purified by You. Help me stand for truth so others will notice You. Amen.

Don't let anyone think less of you because you are young.
Be an example to all believers in what you say, in the way you live,
in your love, your faith, and your purity.
1 TIMOTHY 4:12 NLT

Dear God, You want me to be an example, and being young is a good time to start. You say I can be a great example to other Christians because of my decisions, my love for others, the demonstration of my trust in You, and the way I set myself apart for You. You want me to be pure, and I need You to teach me how. There are so many people who don't think purity is important, and I need friends who will support my choice to be pure. Help me accept Your help to become pure. Amen.

Acknowledge that the LORD is God! He made us. . .we are his people.
PSALM 100:3 NLT

Dear God, You made me, and I am Yours. Sometimes I wonder why I act like I belong to myself. I have always needed help, but instead of letting You help, I do things without Your help, without Your permission, and in a way that doesn't prove that I'm really Yours. Help me always to recognize that You are God and that I exist because You made me. Please purify me and make me a young man who honors, praises, and thanks You. Without You I could not exist. Thanks. Amen.

* * * * * * * * *

"God blesses those whose hearts are pure, for they will see God."
MATTHEW 5:8 NLT

Dear God, You say that the better choices I make, the more I'll understand You. Purity is important to You, so it should be important to me. Whenever I do things my way, it seems You're farther away from me. When I come near to You with a pure heart, You come near to me. When You don't seem close, it's usually because my heart needs the cleaning of forgiveness. When I allow You to clean me up, I understand what You want me to do a little better. I want to be close to You. Amen.

"The human heart is the most deceitful of all things,
and desperately wicked. Who really knows how bad it is?"
JEREMIAH 17:9 NLT

Dear God, You say I can't trust my heart, and I believe it. My heart is the place where I understand You best, but it's also the place where what I feel causes me to think about things I shouldn't. If my eyes see something that You want to protect me from, it's possible my heart will accept flawed feelings instead of truth. Your words call my heart desperately wicked and deceitful. My heart is so complex that the only one who understands it is You. Thanks for continuing to rescue me from an impure heart. Amen.

* * * * * * * * *

Wash me clean from my guilt. Purify me from my sin.
PSALM 51:2 NLT

Dear God, You say I am guilty and I can only agree with You. I make wrong choices even though I know right from wrong. Your words tell me You offer Christians grace. It's this gift that I can use to gain forgiveness and freedom. Instead of just asking You to forgive, I want to welcome the idea of change. I shouldn't stay the same. I've had the habit of sinning because I know You'll forgive. Help me make better choices, because I want to stay close to You. Wash me, purify me, and keep me close. Amen.

Dear friends, we are already God's children, but he has not yet shown us what we will be like when Christ appears. But we do know that we will be like him, for we will see him as he really is. And all who have this eager expectation will keep themselves pure, just as he is pure.
1 JOHN 3:2–3 NLT

Dear God, because You're coming back, You want me to keep myself pure while I wait. I know *You're* pure and You're my living example. When You come back, Your words say that I will be like You. Everything about me will be different then. When I have hope that I will see You, I will want to make right choices, Maybe that's because I don't want to be embarrassed when You arrive. I want to be pure because You are pure. I want to look forward to seeing You. I want to be Your faithful, pure servant. Amen.

* * * * * * * * *

Purify me from my sins, and I will be clean; wash me, and I will be whiter than snow.
PSALM 51:7 NLT

Dear God, You want me to understand that only You can purify my heart, and only You can make me clean. It's not because I try hard. It's not because I do more good things than bad. It's not because people recognize me as a nice guy. I'm clean because You make me clean. I'm pure only because Jesus paid the price for my sin. I can be clean. I can experience purity, but only because of You. When I make right choices, I'm saying thank You, and I'm proving I want to *stay* close to You. Amen.

(Jesus said,) "Pray like this: Our Father in heaven, may your name be kept holy. May your Kingdom come soon. May your will be done on earth, as it is in heaven. Give us today the food we need, and forgive us our sins, as we have forgiven those who sin against us. And don't let us yield to temptation, but rescue us from the evil one."

MATTHEW 6:9–13 NLT

Dear God, Your Son taught me how to pray. I should thank You, think of what it will be like to be with You, ask for Your plans to come true, thank You for food, ask for forgiveness, and ask for Your help so that when I'm tempted I don't sin as You rescue me from evil. The way You ask me to pray has everything to do with seeking to live a life where purity is valued. Protect my eyes, hands, feet, mouth, heart, and mind. Then purify everything else. Help me seek You above all. Amen.

MY PURPOSE—THE POWER OF FOLLOWING THE LEADER

God made you to be more than a guy who wears a uniform, carries a ball, and celebrates a collection of points. You were created for more than outdoor quests or indoor gaming. You were created for great adventure, revolutionary thinking, and an amazing journey with God.

If what you choose to think and do ignores God, then you're missing out on some of the most important moments in life.

God isn't confined to a weekend church event or a few minutes a day reading or thinking about Him. He doesn't just hang out at youth group waiting to be noticed. God is working all the time, and He invites you to work with Him. It might be sweaty work, or it could be discovering a new friend who needs to know God.

God has always known how to lead, but we aren't always good followers. We may think of God as a great adviser, but He wants to be our Leader. He doesn't just give bits of wisdom. He invites you to obey His instructions so that when the next great adventure arrives, you are prepared, excited, and ready to follow.

Let us strip off every weight that slows us down, especially the sin that so easily trips us up. And let us run with endurance the race God has set before us. We do this by keeping our eyes on Jesus, the champion who initiates and perfects our faith.
HEBREWS 12:1–2 NLT

Dear God, You gave me a race to run, and You don't want anything to slow me down. This happens when I'm distracted, tired, overwhelmed, and discouraged. There's one thing that will test my endurance every time—sin. Your words say that sin trips me today and slows me down in the future. You want me to keep my eyes on Jesus. He's a coach teaching me how to run, what to avoid, and how to get back up when I fall. He teaches me what faith is and keeps improving my faith skills. Help me run with You. Amen.

> "I know the plans I have for you," says the LORD. "They are plans for good and not for disaster, to give you a future and a hope."
> JEREMIAH 29:11 NLT

Dear God, You didn't create me and then wonder what I would be able to do. You had a plan, a purpose, and a hope for what I could become. There was never a question in Your mind that I could be useful, but when I refuse to cooperate with Your plans, then the good things I might have accomplished are left undone. It must be annoying when You have plans for me and I refuse to follow. Help me follow You, because if You have plans for me, I want to know what they are. Amen.

* * * * * * * * *

> Take no part in the worthless deeds of evil and darkness; instead, expose them.
> EPHESIANS 5:11 NLT

Dear God, You want me to stay away from evil but expose it for what it really is. Pointing out the bad things around me can seem hard, because not everyone will agree with me. That's why I need to spend time learning from You. I can't argue with Your words. What You have to say puts a spotlight on truth so I can recognize things that are false. Without Your words, I will be unsure what is truth and what should be avoided. Help me always to discover truth by spending time with You. Amen.

All Scripture is inspired by God and is useful to teach us what is true and to make us realize what is wrong in our lives. It corrects us when we are wrong and teaches us to do what is right.
2 TIMOTHY 3:16 NLT

Dear God, You have a plan for teaching me truth. Your words are not just suggestions, but a road map for my life journey. Your words teach truth, correct mistakes, and help me make right choices. You didn't say something and then change Your mind. You explain truth and then ask me to do the right thing. You never ask me if I feel like obeying, You just want me to obey. Your Word will always point to the things that prove I have not followed You well. You promised to lead. Help me to walk with You. Amen.

* * * * * * * * *

Jesus Christ is the same yesterday, today, and forever.
HEBREWS 13:8 NLT

Dear God, Your words are an excellent source for discovering each new step I should take in my journey into the future with You. I don't have to worry, because You never change. What You want from Your family hasn't changed. Your love for me has never weakened. Your faithfulness to me has never depended on how faithful I am to You. Although I might change attitudes and opinions on a regular basis, You never do. Help me find comfort in knowing that You are dependable, honorable, and faithful. Amen.

When I was a child, I spoke and thought and reasoned as a child.
But when I grew up, I put away childish things.
1 CORINTHIANS 13:11 NLT

Dear God, You want me to stop acting like a spiritual child. Your words say that You love children and know they have a greater ability to believe in You, but when I came to accept Your great gifts of salvation, forgiveness, and eternal life, I needed to grow up in You. It's a wonderful thing to accept the good gifts You offer, but You have plans for me that will force me to grow up and to stop acting like someone who doesn't believe that following You is important. Help me become more like You every day. Amen.

* * * * * * * * *

We will speak the truth in love,
growing in every way more and more like Christ.
EPHESIANS 4:15 NLT

Dear God, You gave a great example of what it's like to speak the truth while loving others. I may not feel comfortable telling the truth because it might make that person sad. If I'm supposed to follow You, then sharing truth is important. When I tell someone the truth but don't love them, the truth can seem cruel. When I love someone but don't tell the truth, I am lying. Love plus truth means that even if it's difficult I will tell the truth because I care about others. Help me grow more like You. Amen.

Take a new grip with your tired hands and strengthen your weak knees.
Mark out a straight path for your feet so that those who are weak
and lame will not fall but become strong.
HEBREWS 12:12–13 NLT

Dear God, You ask me to be a trailblazer, and You promise it will
be hard work. This promise seems hard. I like easier promises
like Your love, forgiveness, and grace. You want me to do the hard
work of following You and making sure others have an example to
follow. Your words say I will use tired hands and weak knees, but
I will follow a course, mark a trail, and invite others to follow. We
can encourage each other as we keep heading toward the end of
our journey. Thanks for giving the strength that I need. Amen.

Loving God means keeping his commandments,
and his commandments are not burdensome.
1 JOHN 5:3 NLT

Dear God, You want me to show how much I love You by obeying Your commands. I don't want to be someone who says I follow You but will only do what I want. When Your words show me something I should obey but I don't like what You've commanded, I need to change the way I look at things. Help me see Your plans as a way to show how much You love me and my obedience as my way of showing how much I love You. You have always been worth following. Amen.

* * * * * * * * *

God blesses those who patiently endure testing and temptation.
Afterward they will receive the crown of life that God
has promised to those who love him.
JAMES 1:12 NLT

Dear God, You want me to be patient when I go through tests. You want me to live through temptations without giving in. When I succeed, You call me blessed. You have a gift for me in heaven if I patiently wait for Your help without giving up. Your words tell me that Jesus lived through many tests and temptations. He was patient and finished the work You gave Him by paying the sin debt for everyone on a cross. Give me the courage and patience to endure. That's what it looks like to love You. Amen.

> **Don't act thoughtlessly,
> but understand what the Lord wants you to do.**
> EPHESIANS 5:17 NLT

Dear God, Your greatest desire for me is to follow You with all that I am. When I make decisions without asking for Your wisdom, I'm choosing to follow my own path instead of the one You created for me. Your words are the right place for me to go whenever I need to understand the next step in my God journey. You have things You want me to do, but if I refuse to ask for Your wisdom or seek answers in Your words, I become a fool. Help me understand Your commands. Amen.

* * * * * * * * *

> **The wisdom of this world is foolishness to God.**
> 1 CORINTHIANS 3:19 NLT

Dear God, You want me to know that when I think I'm smart I might actually be acting foolish. The world around me thinks of how to get ahead, strategies for success, and ways to win. People who need help are overlooked, the unnoticed stay that way, and people without hope are left alone to keep looking. You choose people like me to help others even when it seems like I should only look out for my own interests. If this way of thinking is foolishness to You, then make it seem foolish to me, because I follow You. Amen.

> As you endure this divine discipline, remember that God
> is treating you as his own children. Who ever heard of a child
> who is never disciplined by its father?
> HEBREWS 12:7 NLT

Dear God, You want me to understand that I will be disciplined as I follow Your lead. Your words say that You correct us because the best fathers always guide their children. It's not fun being corrected. But because I have chosen to follow You, I must remember that You will always treat me as a member of Your family. If I'm off course, then I should expect to be moved back in the right direction. You call what You do *divine discipline*, and love is the reason for correction. Help me endure for my good and Your honor. Amen.

* * * * * * * *

> Three things will last forever—faith, hope, and love—
> and the greatest of these is love.
> 1 CORINTHIANS 13:13 NLT

Dear God, You want my future filled with things that endure. I won't take stuff with me when I go to heaven. Cars, houses, and money won't go with me. However, the things You say will endure are things that can follow me. I can take my faith, hope, and love. My sharing these three gifts with others will enable them to learn more about You. I can't take stuff, but I can always take the gifts You give. These are gifts that no matter how much I give away I always have enough. Help me share Your gifts. Amen.

Let us think of ways to motivate one another to acts of love and good
works. And let us not neglect our meeting together,
as some people do, but encourage one another.
HEBREWS 10:24–25 NLT

Dear God, You want me to encourage others to love You. Part
of my job is making sure others know I believe You're worth
following. You want me to use my mind to think of interesting
ways to help others see that loving people and helping out when
someone needs help is a regular part of my journey with You. I
should also get together with other Christians. That's what church
is all about, but I can also meet with others at school, youth group,
or at home. We all need encouragement. Help me follow You by
encouraging others. Amen.

MY RESPECT—
THE POWER OF HONOR

Have you ever been bullied? Have you ever been a bully? God wants you to stand up to a bully–even if it's yourself.

Bullies hurt others because they don't know the right way to respond. When they don't feel they have choices, they want control. When they want control, it's easy to do hurtful things they regret.

If you're a bully, God wants you to stop. If you're being bullied, you have choices you'll need to make.

Use kind words, look for a peaceful solution, love others, ask an adult for help, and remember God made you new when you accepted His best gifts. You're supposed to be different.

Bullies can look cruel but may be hurting inside. You can help them even when it seems they're not interested.

If we all make the choice to repay every mean action with another mean action, then we are forgetting God's forgiveness and refusing to show His love, and we'll never offer a glimpse at a better future.

Without Jesus we all would be bullies. He helps us choose a new response.

(Jesus said,) "You have heard the law that says,
'Love your neighbor' and hate your enemy. But I say,
love your enemies! Pray for those who persecute you!"
MATTHEW 5:43—44 NLT

Dear God, You've given me a powerful tool to use when I struggle
to deal with a bully—prayer. You tell me to love my enemies. I
can't do that without Your help. It's easy to think that other people
should pay for bad choices. It's easy to believe I can only love nice
people. It's much harder to care about people who hurt others.
Maybe You tell me to love and pray for my enemies because You
want to make them my friends. Even if they don't change, maybe
You can change my thinking. Amen.

> If anyone claims, "I am living in the light," but hates a fellow believer,
> that person is still living in darkness.
> 1 John 2:9 NLT

Dear God, You tell me to live in the light. This is where I understand You better, see Your plans more clearly, and learn what You can do with someone like me. I like this place. It pulls me closer to You. I like telling others that I'm close to You, too. But when I choose not to love another Christian, it means I'm not as close to You as I should be. It makes me a bully. I can't hate other people and stay close to You. Help me choose Your love and light over hate and darkness. Amen.

* * * * * * * * *

> Some people make cutting remarks,
> but the words of the wise bring healing.
> Proverbs 12:18 NLT

Dear God, You always have a right response when bad things happen. When I want to get back at someone, You remind me that kindness is better than being cruel, respect is better than dishonor, and love is better than hate. Sometimes I have been mean to someone who was mean to me first. That's a choice that's easy to make, but it's not Your choice. Your wise words always help me learn, grow, and make better decisions. When people say or do mean things, help me always to remember what You think of me. Amen.

Oh, the joys of those who do not follow the advice of the wicked,
or stand around with sinners, or join in with mockers.
But they delight in the law of the LORD.
PSALM 1:1—2 NLT

Dear God, You make it clear that I've been given a choice. Following You is something I can decide to do every day. I could follow bad advice. I could spend time with people who don't love You. I could make fun of You with a group of people who have made a choice not to follow You. Help me rediscover the joy of really following—every day. Making bad choices is easy, because someone is always cheering me on. Help me make the right choices for Your honor and my future. Amen.

* * * * * * * * *

Don't use foul or abusive language. Let everything you say
be good and helpful, so that your words will be an
encouragement to those who hear them.
EPHESIANS 4:29 NLT

Dear God, Your words say that my choice of words shows what's really going on in my heart. When I use words to hurt people, my heart might just be on a journey away from Your footsteps. When I use good, helpful, and encouraging words, I express a heart that understands that the way You care for me is a picture of what it should look like for me to care for others. My choice of words can make me a bully or a trusted friend. I know what You'd want. Help me be very careful with my words. Amen.

> Turn away from evil and do good. Search for peace,
> and work to maintain it.
> PSALM 34:14 NLT

Dear God, You want me to hunt for peace, and when I find it I should work hard to protect it. I can do this with Your help and by turning away from things like chaos, anger, and violence that don't get along well with peace. When a bully tries to make me mad, I need to remember how hard I've worked for personal peace and then choose a better response. When people choose peace over violence, the result is a powerful statement that You have a better way for us to live. Amen.

* * * * * * * *

> Don't be selfish; don't try to impress others. Be humble,
> thinking of others as better than yourselves.
> PHILIPPIANS 2:3 NLT

Dear God, You want me to be humble. Bullies can't be humble, because that would mean thinking of others as more important than they are. If other people are that important, then bullies would honor them instead of hurting them. Bullies are selfish and try to impress others through what they do to make people look bad. Help me refuse to treat bullies badly. It can be easy to become a bully if I try to make them pay. Keep me humble. Help me honor You and Your words that bring life. Amen.

There are six things the LORD hates—no, seven things he detests: haughty eyes, a lying tongue, hands that kill the innocent, a heart that plots evil, feet that race to do wrong, a false witness who pours out lies, a person who sows discord in a family.
PROVERBS 6:16–19 NLT

Dear God, You gave me a list of things You hate. This must be important, because You loved me enough to send Jesus to save me. If I were to look at the opposite of this list, maybe it would show the love You want from me. I should have a humble heart, a voice that speaks the truth in love, hands that protect the innocent, a heart that longs for good, feet that race to help, a witness that speaks honestly, and someone who seeks harmony in his family. With Your help I can become this man. Amen.

> The LORD is close to the brokenhearted;
> he rescues those whose spirits are crushed.
> PSALM 34:18 NLT

Dear God, You know how to help when someone is mean to me. Before I was born, You knew that someone would be unkind to me. Before I was ever picked on, You knew that mean words and unkind actions would leave me feeling crushed. Because You know everything, You made a decision to come close to remind me that no matter how mean people can be, You have always loved me and You have something very special for me to do. Help me run to You, because I don't think I can face this alone. Amen.

* * * * * * * * *

> The LORD watches over the path of the godly,
> but the path of the wicked leads to destruction.
> PSALM 1:6 NLT

Dear God, because I walk with You I can be sure You pay attention to every step I take. I feel badly for those who choose to walk a wicked path. The journey of my life starts and ends with a path. Your words say that *Your* path leads to eternal life, forgiveness, and You. The other path only promises destruction in a place where You do not live. Watch over me. Help me follow Your path. Guide my steps. Heal my heart. Help others see that Your honor is more important than destructive choices. Amen.

> Rescue the poor and helpless;
> deliver them from the grasp of evil people.
> PSALM 82:4 NLT

Dear God, You're ready to rescue at a moment's notice. Bullies aren't just mean kids at school. There are people who take other people hostage. Some are kidnapped and held for ransom. You want me to follow Your example and care for those who need help. My first response is to pray that You would rescue the poor and helpless. That's my prayer for the kids I know and people around the world who need Your help right now. Amen.

* * * * * * * * *

> Love each other with genuine affection,
> and take delight in honoring each other.
> ROMANS 12:10 NLT

Dear God, You want me to find joy in honoring other people. This means I'm happy for them when they do well. This also means that I'm willing to help when they need help. Those who walk with You should be known for their love and not for trying to get their own way. You don't want bullies in Your family. You want people who care about, encourage, and share with each other. Even if other people try to become most important, help me always to follow You. You're the most significant Leader this world will ever know. Amen.

> Be patient in trouble, and keep on praying.
> **ROMANS 12:12** NLT

Dear God, You want me to know that any trouble I may face will not last forever. You make it clear in Your words that You want me to pray when I face difficult days. Whether it's a bully, a test, or even my health Your help is on the way. I may not see Your answer today, this month, or even this year, but You have a plan, and it always involves patience and prayer. If the answer never arrives in this lifetime, I still can be joyful in knowing that I will not face that problem in heaven. Amen.

* * * * * * * * *

> Don't look out only for your own interests,
> but take an interest in others, too.
> **PHILIPPIANS 2:4** NLT

Dear God, You want me to know that other people are important. I'm pretty good at certain things, and I'm happy when my friends do what I like. If I want to respond the way You respond, then I need to be interested in others. This could mean I learn more about what they like. It will always mean that I let love lead me to ways to care about them. Bullies always want others to think they're the best. You want me to do what is best—and care for others. That's what I want to do. Amen.

If you keep yourself pure, you will be a special utensil for honorable use. Your life will be clean, and you will be ready for the Master to use you for every good work.
2 TIMOTHY 2:21 NLT

Dear God, You want to use people to do good work, but that may be hard for bullies because the choices they make don't match Your character. You love all people—even bullies—but when it's time to use people to do what You command, You want them to be able to follow Your directions. Your words say we should seek to make good choices so we can be ready to be used by You. I will always be imperfect, but when I sin I want to turn back to You and follow You once more. Amen.

MY SALVATION—
THE POWER TO RESCUE MY SOUL

Those who are employed get paid. That's the way we expect things to work, right? When people work hard, they earn money for a job well done.

God does things differently. He has gifts to offer, and He has the ability to rescue us from a sinful past, but He wants us to accept His offer first.

You have to understand you can never work hard enough to earn forgiveness. You can't buy eternal life. You just have to receive forgiveness and life as gifts from the God who loves you. Saying thanks is always a good response. Remember, if you have to work for a gift, then it's not really a gift.

When you ask God to rescue you, He also gives you everything you need to become more like Him. We know when we're really growing because our lives will show it. Galatians 5:22–23 (NLT) says, "The Holy Spirit produces this kind of fruit in our lives: love, joy, peace, patience, kindness, goodness, faithfulness, gentleness, and self-control." When you show this *fruit* in your life, you are showing thankfulness for God's great gifts.

When God our Savior revealed his kindness and love, he saved us, not because of the righteous things we had done, but because of his mercy. He washed away our sins, giving us a new birth and new life through the Holy Spirit.

TITUS 3:4–5 NLT

Dear God, You are merciful. Your mercy shows up when I go to my family and ask for forgiveness after I've done the wrong thing and then feel badly about it. You could punish me, but You forgive me instead. Because I sin by making bad choices, You offered an entirely new life by being kind enough to show mercy and by being loving enough to take an eraser to my list of sins. The only things I know to add to what You give are thankfulness and obedience. Let that be my gift to You. Amen.

Whoever has the Son has life;
whoever does not have God's Son does not have life.
1 JOHN 5:12 NLT

Dear God, You offer life, and I accept that life. You said real life was found in Jesus, and I invite Your Son to allow me to live more like You. Even though some people live without loving Jesus, You say they aren't really living. I am thankful that You offered something more. Life in You makes a difference in me. It makes a difference in how I think of people I meet. It also makes a difference in how I live. Change me, and make me new. Amen.

* * * * * * * * *

For God made Christ, who never sinned, to be the offering for our sin, so that we could be made right with God through Christ.
2 CORINTHIANS 5:21 NLT

Dear God, You paid for something I was responsible to pay. Your words tell me that *everyone* sins. Your words tell me that the only payment I can expect from sin is death. Your words also tell me that Jesus never sinned, so You accepted His sacrifice instead. I'm sad Jesus had to die because I sin, but I am also thankful I can be forgiven and accepted by You because of His gift. Jesus lives, and He lives in me. Amen.

> If we are living in the light, as God is in the light,
> then we have fellowship with each other, and the blood of Jesus,
> his Son, cleanses us from all sin.
> 1 JOHN 1:7 NLT

Dear God, You want me to spend time with those who follow You. I learn from others who have learned from You. Everyone learns best by reading Your words. You bring us together because Jesus paid the price of forgiveness. Help me understand the value of people. You love each of us and offer the same gift to everyone. I don't know why someone would say no to Your gift. It would be awesome if everyone said yes to God. Amen.

* * * * * * * * *

> The Lord isn't really being slow about his promise, as some people
> think. No, he is being patient for your sake. He does not want
> anyone to be destroyed, but wants everyone to repent.
> 2 PETER 3:9 NLT

Dear God, You are patient. Some people think there are too many bad things happening around the world. They wonder why You haven't come back. Some people have waited all their lives for You to return. It's just like You to be patient enough so that people who aren't following You can turn away from being sinful and start to follow. I don't mind waiting to see You if it means more people can accept Your best gifts. Thanks for being patient. Help me to be patient, too. Amen.

"There is salvation in no one else! God has given no other name under heaven by which we must be saved."
ACTS 4:12 NLT

Dear God, You are the ultimate God. No one else even comes close. You told us Jesus rescues us. You also said there was no one else in the entire world who could offer salvation. My sin can only be forgiven because Jesus died on the cross. I can only spend forever with You because Jesus didn't stay dead. Because I want to be with You in heaven, I shouldn't look anywhere else but Jesus to help me understand what I must do to follow You with everything I am. Today I choose to keep following You. Amen.

* * * * * * * *

Just as you accepted Christ Jesus as your Lord, you must continue to follow him.
COLOSSIANS 2:6 NLT

Dear God, You provide the best instructions. You words tell me that I shouldn't just accept Your best gifts and then walk away. Your gifts change lives. Understanding how valuable Your gifts of love, forgiveness, and life really are make me want to learn more about what You want me to do. If You can change my life, my heart, and my thoughts, then You can change anyone. It's as if You asked me to come along on a lifelong adventure and You're the tour guide. Help me be willing to go where You lead. Amen.

"A person is made right with God by faith in Jesus Christ,
not by obeying the law. And we have believed in Christ Jesus,
so that we might be made right with God because of our faith in Christ."
GALATIANS 2:16 NLT

Dear God, You accepted me even when I didn't obey. I know You want me to obey, but Your words say that my connection with You is repaired when I have faith in Your Son, Jesus. To have faith means to really believe, and I have to admit sometimes it's hard to believe in someone I've never seen. But I see the way You care for me when the sun comes up each morning, when my family's needs are met, when I see people who smile. I want to be right with You, so I choose to believe. Amen.

Salvation is not a reward for the good things we have done,
so none of us can boast about it.
EPHESIANS 2:9 NLT

Dear God, You did it all. You didn't need any help. You created this world with nothing but Your imagination. You made people so we could think, make decisions, and build things. Sometimes we think we're more important than You. We think we can *make* You do things for us, but Your words tell us no one can brag, because You came up with the idea of salvation. You said we couldn't earn it. You said salvation is not a reward for good behavior. We can come to You because You came for us. Now that's worth bragging about. Amen.

* * * * * * * * *

For God so loved the world that he gave his one and only Son,
that whoever believes in him shall not perish but have eternal life.
JOHN 3:16 NIV

Dear God, You love me. It doesn't matter if I think I deserve it or not. Your words say You loved me enough to send Your only Son to live on earth for a while. When I should have been punished for my sin, Jesus was punished instead. When I think of how Jesus died, I wish things could have been different, but if Jesus hadn't paid the price, then someday I would have to be punished for my sin, and I could never talk to You as a friend. Thanks for loving me that much. Amen.

Jesus told him, "I am the way, the truth, and the life. No one can come
to the Father except through me."
JOHN 14:6 NLT

Dear God, Your Son offers the only way to repair a soul. He is the
only real truth. If I want real life, I discover it only by finding and
following Him. In fact, I can find You only by finding Jesus. He is
the only reason we can be friends. Jesus knows the way I need to
go. He knows the truth that brings real freedom. He is where true
life begins. Jesus made following easy. Help me stay focused on
the journey ahead. Amen.

* * * * * * * * *

"The Son of Man came to seek and save those who are lost."
LUKE 19:10 NLT

Dear God, You found me. I didn't think I was hiding, but I also
wasn't willing to be found. If I'm truthful, I think You knew where I
was all along, but I kept looking at Your gifts and refused to accept
them. Maybe I thought there would be a catch. Maybe I thought
I wasn't good enough yet. Maybe I thought I would miss out on
something if I spent too much time with You. I was lost. I wasn't
good enough. I was lost, and You loved me anyway. I was never so
happy to be found. Amen.

> If you openly declare that Jesus is Lord and believe in your heart that
> God raised him from the dead, you will be saved.
> ROMANS 10:9 NLT

Dear God, Your Son is alive. Because He lives, I have been rescued. It's easy to say I love Jesus when it's pretty clear He loved me first. He died and rose again long before I was even born, but Your words tell me that even then You knew me. My brain is convinced, my heart trusts, and my mouth should always be willing to be talk about Jesus, the One who saves. He has plans, He knows the way, and He wants me to follow. Your Son has always been the best Leader. Amen.

* * * * * * * *

> "Everyone who calls on the name of the LORD will be saved."
> ROMANS 10:13 NLT

Dear God, You make it easy to be saved. If I call on the name of the Lord, I can be rescued, and I have a right to use all Your gifts. I can always ask for Your help. You don't keep salvation away from anyone. No matter where I came from, my family name, or my skin color, You said I was part of the *everyone* who could call on You for rescue. When I called, You answered. That was a good day. Amen.

Christ suffered for our sins once for all time. He never sinned, but he died for sinners to bring you safely home to God. He suffered physical death, but he was raised to life in the Spirit.

1 PETER 3:18 NLT

Dear God, Your Son, Jesus, paid for my sin by dying on a cross. His gift was so perfect; it was the only sacrifice He would have to make to save me from all the sinful things I have ever done. His sacrifice was also enough to save anyone who asks. He came back to life after three days and returned to God. Jesus wanted all of us to become Your friends. He wanted all of us to spend forever with You in heaven. He wants to take me to see You. He's one amazing Son. I'm glad I know Him. Amen.

MY SERVICE—
THE POWER OF INITIATIVE

Have you ever wondered if a Christian needs to do acts of service for God? After all, God made everything and keeps everything working. What can you do that He couldn't do Himself? Wouldn't He do a better job?

These are good questions, but they're the wrong questions to ask. It's not because God can't do something that He asks us to work. It's because He created us with skills that need to be developed to help other people. Acts of service do that.

We work because it brings us closer to the things that are important to God. We will be asked to be kind, loving, courageous, helpful, honest, and strong.

Your parents may ask you to do things around the house. They may be able do the work themselves, but you won't learn anything staring at a computer screen trying to nab wayward mutant warthogs on the streets of Chicago if they do. Our work helps us learn and grow, and it helps others see the value of learning and growing.

When we do what needs to be done, we help others see the value of a God worth serving.

"Whoever wants to be first among you must be the slave of everyone else. For even the Son of Man came not to be served but to serve others and to give his life as a ransom for many."

MARK 10:44–45 NLT

Dear God, You didn't just tell me to serve. You sent Your Son, Jesus, to show me what it looks like to serve You well. He didn't demand that people serve Him. He washed the disciples' feet, He calmed storms, and then He gave up His life by dying on a cross. I wouldn't even have a chance to talk to You if Jesus hadn't come to serve. I shouldn't try to be noticed by others when I serve You. I should serve because it shows that Your words and Your ideas are changing my mind and my heart. Amen.

> "You should remember the words of the Lord Jesus:
> 'It is more blessed to give than to receive.' "
> ACTS 20:35 NLT

Dear God, You want me to know that whenever I give I receive a blessing. You never say in Your words what that blessing is, but I know when I give with a good attitude I feel like I have done something important. Maybe that's Your blessing. I don't want to give wondering what I'll get. I want to give because I love You and I know that You gave me everything I have. I can serve You by sharing some of my time and some of my money. Help me find ways to serve You because I love You. Amen.

* * * * * * * *

> Use your freedom to serve one another in love.
> GALATIANS 5:13 NLT

Dear God, You created me to be free enough to do what You made me to do. Serving someone else is supposed to be the result of the love You have always offered me. I should show Your love to others in everything I do. Looking at serving others as something that interrupts the things I want doesn't help me understand that the love You want me to share comes from a God who is interrupted daily with requests to help people just like me. You don't complain. Help me serve with patience. Amen.

*The generous will prosper; those who refresh others
will themselves be refreshed.*
PROVERBS 11:25 NLT

Dear God, You don't want prosperity and refreshment to be the main reason I obey Your command to serve and give. When all I want is Your rewards, then what I do for others seems like a job and what You do for me seems more like a paycheck. When I give, it should be because I want to share from a thankful heart. When I serve, it should be because I love being part of Your family, and working together should be normal. Help me never look at serving as just a way to earn Your gifts. Amen.

* * * * * * * * *

(Jesus said,) "You are my friends if you do what I command."
JOHN 15:14 NLT

Dear God, when You told Your disciples that they were Your friends, that was pretty special. Being a friend of God is an honor. You also told them that they should do what You asked them to do. Your words tell us that we can grow up as Christians when we become more like You by reading Your words and doing what You say. I couldn't play football if I didn't know the rules. If I didn't follow the rules, I'd spend time on the bench. Help me be a friend who does what You say I should do. Amen.

> My dear brothers and sisters, be strong and immovable.
> Always work enthusiastically for the Lord, for you know
> that nothing you do for the Lord is ever useless.
> 1 CORINTHIANS 15:58 NLT

Dear God, You say that everything I do for You is important even if I think it might not be worthwhile. You say my attitude is important. You want me to serve enthusiastically. Maybe that's because I get to serve the God who made me. When I think about how awesome You are, it is amazing that You have something for me to do for You. That makes it easy to say yes. Help me be strong. Help me stick to the task You have for me. Help me serve to the best of my ability. Amen.

* * * * * * * * *

> Don't just listen to God's word. You must do what it says.
> Otherwise, you are only fooling yourselves.
> JAMES 1:22 NLT

Dear God, You don't want me to believe a lie. When I think that I can read Your words or listen to them spoken by someone else but I don't have to obey, I fool myself into believing that Your words aren't important. It's almost like saying I'm smarter than You—and I'm not. You want me to obey. I must take action. I have stuff to do. It's simple. I should learn what You've said and then do what You say. You're God. What You say is not foolish. Help me obey Your words. Amen.

Dear brothers and sisters, I plead with you to give your bodies to God because of all he has done for you. Let them be a living and holy sacrifice—the kind he will find acceptable. This is truly the way to worship him.

ROMANS 12:1 NLT

Dear God, You want me to worship You in what I do. You're amazing, and what I do is important to You. You want me to offer all of me so I can grow up to act like You. Your words say I'm to give You my body as a living and holy sacrifice. You want to keep my body pure so You can use it to do the things You made me to do. When I cooperate, You say that You accept my gift. Help me worship You with all of me. Amen.

> I am not ashamed of this Good News about Christ. It is the power
> of God at work, saving everyone who believes.
> ROMANS 1:16 NLT

Dear God, You have the most amazing news, and You want me to share it with everyone I know. I don't want to be ashamed of that news or the effect it can have on people I know. This news explains that You're hard at work saving everyone who believes that You loved them enough to accept Your Son's (Jesus) sacrifice for all the sins anyone will ever carry out. This is Your news. I am just someone who shares Your story. Help me see the power of Your message and communicate Your Good News without being embarrassed. Amen.

* * * * * * * * *

> Work willingly at whatever you do, as though you were
> working for the Lord rather than for people.
> COLOSSIANS 3:23 NLT

Dear God, You want me to know that no matter what chore I am asked to do You're the only one I should try to please. That means that if I'm asked to take out the trash, I want to make sure I do the best job possible because I want to honor You in everything. Sometimes that means I do even more than is expected because I am working for You. Whenever I work, it's important because the result of my best efforts should always be dedicated to You. Help me work—for You. Amen.

Remember that the Lord will give you an inheritance as your reward, and that the Master you are serving is Christ.
COLOSSIANS 3:24 NLT

Dear God, You have a gift to give, and I will always be part of an important family when I accept it. Most people receive an inheritance from a family member who dies, but You want to give me an inheritance right now, because You're living. I can have a future with You because You give me the inheritance of being Your child today. When I accepted the pure sacrifice of Your Son, Jesus, I became part of Your family, and I will serve the rest of my life as Your child. Thanks for great gifts. Amen.

*   *   *   *   *   *   *   *   *

Lazy people want much but get little, but those who work hard will prosper.
PROVERBS 13:4 NLT

Dear God, You think hard work is valuable. You say in Your words that people who work hard will flourish. That makes me think of a flower. When it has good soil, sunshine, and water, it becomes something much better than a single seed. When I work hard using the skills You provide, the body You've given me, and the desire to honor You, the end result is so much more than when I started. Help me serve and then work hard so I can finish knowing I did my best. Amen.

Even children are known by the way they act,
whether their conduct is pure, and whether it is right.
PROVERBS 20:11 NLT

Dear God, You pay attention to the way I act. Because You want me to serve in the way Jesus served, I should carefully choose to do things in a way that shows the world You're my God. People can see the way I act, and they'll decide if what I do matches who I'm supposed to be. You ask me to be responsible because other people need to know You. My actions either invite them to learn more or cause them to believe You can't really make a difference. Help me to represent You well. Amen.

* * * * * * * * *

(Jesus said,) "Anyone who wants to be my disciple must follow me,
because my servants must be where I am. And the Father
will honor anyone who serves me."
JOHN 12:26 NLT

Dear God, You want me to follow where You lead. Serving You is what a disciple does. Being a disciple means following You, serving You, and learning from You. If I say I love You but refuse to go where You lead, then I'm not showing I care enough to obey. If I won't obey, then I'm not letting You grow me into the godly man You want me to be one day. Because Your words say You have a plan for my life, please keep me close, help me learn, and give me the desire to follow. Amen.

Take a lesson from the ants, you lazybones. Learn from their ways and become wise! Though they have no prince or governor or ruler to make them work, they labor hard all summer, gathering food for the winter.
PROVERBS 6:6–8 NLT

Dear God, You created ants to share a lesson in how work should be done. They don't have bosses telling them what to do, but they always work hard. When winter comes, they have enough food. This is an example for me to follow. You want me to see work as a way to prepare for my future. You want me to see work as something I do to honor You. You want me to see work as honorable. When I learn Your lessons, Your words say I am becoming wise. Help me to keep learning to follow You. Amen.

MY SCHOOL—
THE POWER OF EDUCATION

You might go to school with lots of other people in a building, or you might go to school with a brother or sister in your living room. You might even attend a Christian or charter school. These are all places where you can learn, but they aren't the only places. School should be wherever you are.

Learning is available when visiting a museum, going for a walk, or taking swimming lessons. Instruction can take place at the kitchen table, Sunday school class, or the zoo. Education should happen outside the classroom.

Your mom or dad might give regular instruction. That's probably why God tells you to honor them. If you do it right, you will continue learning every day for the rest of your life. If that sounds boring, then you probably don't understand the real amazement in learning. Give it time; you might change your mind.

Some of the things we learn help us learn even more. Some things we learn will be interesting. Some things will be difficult to understand. Some things will be amusing. While education changes our minds, godly instruction changes our hearts, our lives, and our futures.

The LORD says, "I will guide you along the best pathway for your life. I will advise you and watch over you."
PSALM 32:8 NLT

Dear God, You protect me. Good teachers make sure their students can learn in a protected environment. You never said that following You would be easy, but You have offered to guide me, be my life adviser, and keep an eye on me as I journey with You. Nothing can happen to me without You knowing it. Your words tell me You always make sure I can see clearly enough to take the next step. Guide me, advise me, and watch over me as I take steps toward You and away from the person I used to be. Amen.

Get all the advice and instruction you can,
so you will be wise the rest of your life.
PROVERBS 19:20 NLT

Dear God, You want me to use my mind. You want the truth I learn to change the way I think, act, and respond to You and others. You don't want me just to know facts. You want me to take what I know and use it for good. What I learn can help me honor my parents, obey Your commands, and help my friends. Because You want me to learn for the rest of my life, help me find ways to learn more about You today so that tomorrow I might be a little bit more like You. Amen.

✳ ✳ ✳ ✳ ✳ ✳ ✳ ✳ ✳

Take hold of my instructions; don't let them go.
Guard them, for they are the key to life.
PROVERBS 4:13 NLT

Dear God, You want me to be a guardian of wise teaching. You have a lot to say in the Bible. The things You say are called the "key to life." When I read Your words, it's like unlocking wisdom I can use to make good decisions. Teach me in Your "God school" and let me hold on to Your instructions for life. Help me know when I should share the things I learn. Help me be brave in sharing them. Help me never leave the truth found in Your words. Amen.

How much better to get wisdom than gold,
and good judgment than silver!
PROVERBS 16:16 NLT

Dear God, do You know how much gold is worth? A lot. Your words tell me Your wisdom is worth even more. People who are wise not only know things, but they are really good at knowing how to handle difficult situations. It's not just that they are smart; they can help people understand things without getting mad. People who have good judgment know when to stay away from something that might cause trouble. I want wisdom and good judgment. Help me find these treasures only You can provide. Amen.

* * * * * * * * *

Wise people treasure knowledge,
but the babbling of a fool invites disaster.
PROVERBS 10:14 NLT

Dear God, You know the difference between knowledge and foolishness. Would You help me learn the difference? Your school is the best place to learn things that are true and honorable. Sometimes I say things I think are true but I didn't really understand, and then I look foolish. Sometimes what I say can hurt other people. I don't want to hurt others. Help me see my time with You as a treasure. Help me to learn and to use what I learn to speak wise words. Amen.

> Intelligent people are always ready to learn.
> Their ears are open for knowledge.
> PROVERBS 18:15 NLT

Dear God, You really want me to learn. When my teachers have something to share, help me to listen. When my Sunday school teacher shares from Your wise words, help me to pay attention. When my mom or dad want to teach me something, help me to be an enthusiastic learner. Because I can learn anywhere, help me to look for chances to learn. That could be a new game, math skill, or ways to serve You better. If intelligent people are always ready to learn, then help me be intelligent. Amen.

* * * * * * * * *

> Instruct the wise, and they will be even wiser.
> PROVERBS 9:9 NLT

Dear God, You know everything. I might know some things, but there's no one as wise as You. I want to be a lot wiser than I am right now. If I am willing to learn, then maybe I can learn even more than I had planned. If I take initiative and read Your words often, then the Bible says I will learn more. With You as my Teacher, I really believe I can learn and grow. What I learn could change me for the better. Your instruction can make me wise. I am Your student. Amen.

Lead me by your truth and teach me, for you are the God
who saves me. All day long I put my hope in you.
PSALM 25:5 NLT

Dear God, You can do it all. You rescue people from sinful lives.
You inspire hope in people who have none. You lead me and teach
me, but I need to recognize that Your words in the Bible are more
than inspirational thoughts—they are truth. You didn't just want
to give me life suggestions. When I am a student of Your truth, I
become more like You, love others in a way that honors You, and
learn in a way that make makes me a modern disciple. May my
choice to learn change me. Amen

> Let the wise listen to these proverbs and become even wiser.
> Let those with understanding receive guidance.
> PROVERBS 1:5 NLT

Dear God, Your guidance is better than a map. Your words say that if I want to be wise, I have to start with understanding. When You teach me, help me understand what You're saying. I may have questions once I begin to understand, but You promise to guide me in the best way. You begin by teaching me, and then You show me ways to use what I am learning. It seems like wisdom is knowing the right thing to do and then knowing how to do the right thing the right way. That's what I want. Amen.

* * * * * * * * *

> Fear of the LORD is the foundation of wisdom.
> Knowledge of the Holy One results in good judgment.
> PROVERBS 9:10 NLT

Dear God, can You help me understand what Jesus would do? I want good judgment. I want to be able to know when I should leave a situation that does not honor You. I want to be able to know the best ways to help other people. I want to know how to show my parents that I love and respect them. Help me know You more. Help me love You deeply. Help me find wisdom by searching for You with my heart, mind, soul, and strength. Amen.

How can a young person stay pure? By obeying your word.
PSALM 119:9 NLT

Dear God, You want me to be pure. Every day I want to learn more about You. Every day I want to learn from You. Every day I want to honor You by obeying the things I know You want from me. I may not know everything, but as I attend Your school, I have gained an education that lets me know there are things I should do and things I should avoid. Because I want You to continue teaching me, I want to obey. Give me strength because sometimes it is really hard to do the right thing. Amen.

* * * * * * * * *

Show me the right path, O LORD;
point out the road for me to follow.
PSALM 25:4 NLT

Dear God, You already know the way that leads to my best future. It's awesome to think that following You can lead to the life I was made to live. This is why I need to learn from You. This is why I need to obey. This is why I ask for directions. Every day I face choices. Every choice leads me closer to You or farther away from You. I want the wisdom to recognize the way You lead. I want to be right in the middle of the best things You have planned for me. Amen.

I will study your commandments and reflect on your ways.
PSALM 119:15 NLT

Dear God, You want me to be teachable. For on-the-job training, I need to see how other trusted Christians handle tough problems. When learning directly from You, I need to love Your words. I can find out more about the qualities that make You so different from anyone else I know. I want to learn the things You ask me to do. Then when I study, I need to spend time thinking about how what I have learned can change who I am. Really knowing God changes something inside. Please change me. Amen.

* * * * * * * *

If you need wisdom, ask our generous God, and he will give it to you. He will not rebuke you for asking.
JAMES 1:5 NLT

Dear God, You never get mad when I'm confused. I need wisdom, so I'm respectfully asking You for understanding. You love giving good gifts, and wisdom is one of the best. Sometimes it's easy to be confused because Your wisdom is so different than what I know. You want me to love those who hate me, forgive those who hurt me, and give when I don't have much. I'm pretty certain You have good reasons, and that's why I need wisdom. Thanks for being willing to teach me. Help me to understand and obey. Amen.

Fear of the LORD is the foundation of true knowledge,
but fools despise wisdom and discipline.
PROVERBS 1:7 NLT

Dear God, Your instructions require obedience. In school my
teacher will ask me to complete an assignment. It doesn't work
very well if I tell my teacher I just didn't feel like doing the
assignment. He expects me to finish my work. If I don't, then I get
a bad grade. You expect me to obey Your instructions, too. I need
to start by first understanding that everything You do is awesome.
There is nothing You do that is less than awesome. Let me learn
and become wise. Help me be self-controlled enough to complete
Your assignments. Amen.

MY STORY—
THE POWER OF COURAGE

Did you know you have a story that God wants you to share? The story isn't about anything you've accomplished, places you've gone, or people you know. Your story is about how You met God and He changed you. Your story is about Jesus who died on the cross so You could be forgiven for all the sin you will ever carry out.

Your story will be *your* story. Because you are created by God and are unique in every way, the story of how you met God will be just as unique. You may be tempted to add to your story if you think it isn't interesting enough, but don't believe it. God can use your story to encourage others to ask God to change them, too. Any story that starts with God is perfect just the way it is.

You will need to be courageous, because telling other people about God can be hard. When you combine your story with God's help, there is no need to worry. Not everyone will believe your story, but those who do may become new members of your *God* family.

> I know the one in whom I trust, and I am sure that he is able to guard what I have entrusted to him until the day of his return.
> 2 TIMOTHY 1:12 NLT

Dear God, You stand guard over everything I have ever trusted You with. I know You, and I am convinced that I can trust You with anything. Some people will tell my secrets. Some love to point out things they don't like about me. Some only pretend to be friends. You deal with me in a very different way. My story includes Your faithfulness. Your story includes Your love for me. Our stories always go together. Someday I get to meet You face-to-face. I can't wait to see the One I've trusted with my own eyes. Amen.

> "This is my command—be strong and courageous! Do not be afraid or discouraged. For the LORD your God is with you wherever you go."
> JOSHUA 1:9 NLT

Dear God, You want me to know that no matter where I go, You go with me. I can say what You want me to say and do what needs to be done because I'm not alone. I don't need to be afraid. I don't need to worry. I don't even need to apologize for speaking the truth. I can tell anyone what You've done for me, because when I share Your love, I share hope. When someone encounters hope, they can believe their future can be different. May I be courageous enough to make a difference. Amen.

* * * * * * * *

> The wicked run away when no one is chasing them,
> but the godly are as bold as lions.
> PROVERBS 28:1 NLT

Dear God, because I believe Your words are true, I don't need to be afraid. Your words say that the people who worry most are those who choose sin over forgiveness. They always wonder when they will be caught. They wonder why they can't be honest. They can't rest. They can't sleep. They find it hard to think clearly. Sometimes I do the same thing. When I'm not following You, I never feel quite right. Maybe those times are reminders that I need to stay close. Make me as bold as a lion. Amen.

171

Wait patiently for the LORD. Be brave and courageous.
Yes, wait patiently for the LORD.
PSALM 27:14 NLT

Dear God, Your words tell me that I become more courageous when I wait for You to show up. I can be brave when I know that I have Your support. I can speak up when it would be easier to be quiet when I know I have protection. You want me to share the story of how I first understood who You are and the amazing way You made sure I can talk to You whenever I need to. I am bold. I am courageous. I am a child of God. That explains it all. Thanks, God. Amen.

* * * * * * * * *

"We cannot stop telling about everything we have seen and heard."
ACTS 4:20 NLT

Dear God, You've done so much for me that I should never stop talking about it. Your words tell me over and over again that the people who were close to You couldn't stop telling other people. The book of Psalms is filled with ways people expressed the joy of sharing the stories of Your love, forgiveness, help, kindness, and faithfulness. I think You share these moments with me so I can remember that there are more stories to hear and more stories to share. I could live my whole life and still have stories to share about You. Amen.

I know the LORD is always with me. I will not be shaken,
for he is right beside me.
PSALM 16:8 NLT

Dear God, You know it is way too easy for me to worry. You know
I need to be brave, because if I don't share my story, some people
may not hear about You today. Telling people about You can be
hard. I can feel like I'm standing in front of a large audience and
can't think of anything to say. Help me remember my story, and
help me with the words You want me to say. Your words say You
are right beside me. That should give me the courage to be Your
storyteller. Amen.

* * * * * * * * *

(Jesus said,) "Everyone who acknowledges me publicly here on earth,
I will also acknowledge before my Father in heaven."
MATTHEW 10:32 NLT

Dear God, You never want me to keep the story of how You
changed me a secret. If I have information about how life can be
better, I should share the news. If I hide, it's like seeing someone
who is hurt and refusing to help them when I know what to do.
I'm not being very responsible when I respond that way. My story
is only possible because of You. If my story were only about me,
it would sound like bragging. When it's about You, it's more like
worship. Let me worship You with my story. Amen.

Fight the good fight for the true faith. Hold tightly to the eternal life to which God has called you, which you have declared so well before many witnesses.

1 Timothy 6:12 NLT

Dear God, You want me to take my commitment to You seriously. Your words say that it is important to let other believers know that I am on a journey with You. Maybe that's because You want me to have other people who will help me pay attention to the path I am walking. When my story includes other people on the same God-sized adventure, then the people I talk to know they don't have to face the journey alone. Help me invite other Christians to my story so we can walk together. Amen.

Come and listen, all you who fear God,
and I will tell you what he did for me.
PSALM 66:16 NLT

Dear God, You want me to share my story with people who already love You. Some people call this a testimony. A testimony is when a person shares facts, and I want to share facts with those who already believe. When I share my story, those who have their own story will be encouraged. When they share their story, I am encouraged. You make each story personal, and the best stories share how You did something that could never happen without Your help. You do all the good stuff. I just share the details. Amen.

* * * * * * * * *

This is what God has testified: He has given us eternal life,
and this life is in his Son.
1 JOHN 5:11 NLT

Dear God, You gave me a great example for sharing my story. Your words say that Your story is about the way You made eternal life possible. Your story is about love, forgiveness, grace, and rescue. Your story is about a gift of life restoration because of the sacrifice offered by Your Son, Jesus. My story will always need to focus on His story. Jesus is the reason I look forward to spending eternity with You. He's the reason my story can talk about forgiveness. He's the reason I can be called Your child. Jesus *is* my story. Amen.

"Let your good deeds shine out for all to see,
so that everyone will praise your heavenly Father."
MATTHEW 5:16 NLT

Dear God, You want my story to include kind actions. My story wouldn't be worth hearing if I said I love Jesus but never do what Jesus does. When I won't help the people You love, then some people won't believe that You really love them. People want to see if my story and my actions look alike. When they don't match, people won't listen to my story and they won't find it easy to believe in You. Help me make Your story a pattern for my life. May what I do help others see You. Amen.

* * * * * * * * *

I have told all your people about your justice.
I have not been afraid to speak out.
PSALM 40:9 NLT

Dear God, You are more than fair. This is a part of my story that others need to know. Some people think You are harsh while others think You don't really care. Your words say that You want people to have time to accept Your gifts. That's fair. I am thankful You gave me time to see the importance of following You. You are patient with me, but You are also just. You ask people to follow, but You are also kind. Your story is so good, it should always encourage me to honor You. Amen.

> Has the LORD redeemed you? Then speak out!
> **PSALM 107:2** NLT

Dear God, You freed me from my sin sentence, so let me open my mouth and talk about it. Family and friends need to know that it's possible to be forgiven, to live without being guilty of breaking Your law, and to talk to You without the fear that they might be punished. My prayers help put my priorities in order. I can speak more clearly to others after I let You know what's on my mind. I am free because of You. Free my lips so I can tell others just how amazing You are. Amen.

* * * * * * * *

> I will proclaim your justice, and I will praise you all day long.
> **PSALM 35:28** NLT

Dear God, You want my story to be filled with honor. You don't want me to treat You like a guy who lives down the street. You invite me to be a friend, but even more importantly You want me to remember You are God. Your words say You are the author of my story. You know how things turn out, so sharing my story with others shows honor for the work You have already done and an eagerness for what's coming next. Let my story be an offering of thankfulness for all You do for me. Amen.

"See, God has come to save me. I will trust in him and not be afraid. The LORD GOD is my strength and my song; he has given me victory."
ISAIAH 12:2 NLT

Dear God, You want me to know that when I fail, You will step in and be strong for me. I can trust You. Saving is something You have always done. You rescue those who are struggling with sin. Your gifts inspire songs. Your strength brings victory. Your compassion leads to trust. You help me speak about You, and when I do, I become more confident in sharing my story. You always bring Your gifts, and I share Your story and how it changed me. The more I share the easier it becomes. Amen.

MY TEMPER—
THE POWER OF SELF-CONTROL

Have you ever wondered why it's so easy to get mad, throw a fit, and say mean things? It's much harder to smile, help others, and be encouraging when you don't feel like it.

Everyone is born selfish. When we're little children, we don't want to share toys. When a baby brother or sister comes home, we don't want to share Mom and Dad. When it's time to decide what to do, we want everybody to think our ideas are the best.

God wants us to be self-controlled. This means we are to be very careful how we respond to those around us. It means that anger shouldn't be our first choice. It means that we choose to share. It means that we look for good in the things others want to do.

Self-control is something God wants us to develop. Self-control is like developing spiritual muscles. It's how we show that God makes it possible to choose better ways to deal with how we feel.

Self-control always starts by letting us make choices. We can choose to get angry or we can choose to forgive. Being self-controlled helps us become more like Jesus.

Make every effort to respond to God's promises. Supplement your faith with a generous provision of moral excellence, and moral excellence with knowledge, and knowledge with self-control, and self-control with patient endurance, and patient endurance with godliness, and godliness with brotherly affection, and brotherly affection with love for everyone.

2 PETER 1:5–7 NLT

Dear God, You said I can love others when I am self-controlled. Your words tell me that when I make right choices, learn from Your words, choose a good response, am patient with others, choose Your way before mine, and care for others, I become someone who can really love people. Your words tell me that the two greatest things I can do are love God and then love everyone else. Help me to be self-controlled so I can really love others the way You love them. Amen.

A person without self-control is like a city with broken-down walls.
PROVERBS 25:28 NLT

Dear God, You want me to cooperate with You. Self-control is one of the best ways I can do that. When I do what I want without learning what You have to say about my choice in Your words, I get myself in trouble. I don't want to be someone who gets angry thinking that things always have to go my way. Everything about my life works better when I choose to control my actions. You have rescued me and let me decide how close I come to being like You through my choices. Help me to choose wisely. Amen.

✳ ✳ ✳ ✳ ✳ ✳ ✳ ✳ ✳

We are instructed to turn from godless living and sinful pleasures. We should live in this evil world with wisdom, righteousness, and devotion to God.
TITUS 2:12 NLT

Dear God, following Your instructions makes me wise. Many people make bad choices. Their decisions hurt themselves and those they love. Your words tell me to turn away from living that way. The best choices, the ones You tell me about in Your words, show me that I should be wise, honorable, and someone who follows You. Following You means I have choices to make. First, I choose not to do certain things You've said are wrong. Second, I choose to do things that would make You pleased. You've given me good instructions. Thanks. Amen.

Don't you realize that in a race everyone runs,
but only one person gets the prize? So run to win!
1 CORINTHIANS 9:24 NLT

Dear God, You want me to run Your race. I want the wisdom to
know how to run well. I don't know anyone who starts a race
wondering how he can make sure he comes in last. The race
You have for me is a race just for me. I don't compete with other
people, because then I might think I'm better—or worse—than
others who run. You want every part of my racing ability to
improve because I'm learning to follow Your coaching. Thanks for
Your example. Watch me run. Amen.

* * * * * * * * *

All athletes are disciplined in their training. They do it to win
a prize that will fade away, but we do it for an eternal prize.
1 CORINTHIANS 9:25 NLT

Dear God, You have created a training program just for me.
I choose to be self-controlled enough to accept training by
reading Your words with a good attitude. Help me choose daily
training. Help me endure hard lessons. Help me put what I learn
to the test. You've agreed to train me. I want to be disciplined
enough to follow through with each test, every struggle. I know
that You will be encouraging me to keep going. With Your help
I can accept the training and run Your race with courage, hope,
and patience. Amen.

Train yourself to be godly.
1 TIMOTHY 4:7 NLT

Dear God, You want me to respond like You. I can never be You, but I should find ways to help people see what You look like. If I am rude, angry, and impatient, then people who know I'm a Christian will wonder if that's what You're like. If I'm kind, joyful, and patient, then people will think of You in a better way—the way You should be thought of. That's the way I want to be. I need the self-control required to be patient enough to show others how awesome You really are. Amen.

* * * * * * * * *

Teach the older men to exercise self-control,
to be worthy of respect, and to live wisely. They must have
sound faith and be filled with love and patience.
TITUS 2:2 NLT

Dear God, You have given me great examples of what self-control looks like. Some examples I see with my own eyes. Others I read about in Your words. You say that people with self-control should be respected. I still need You to help me learn how to be self-controlled, but I am thankful for those who love me and are patient when I blow it. With Your help, I would like to grow up to become someone others can see as an example of what it looks like to follow You. Amen.

Dear friends, never take revenge. Leave that to the righteous anger of God. For the Scriptures say, "I will take revenge; I will pay them back," says the Lord.
ROMANS 12:19 NLT

Dear God, You can take care of everything—even when I want to help. It's easy to get angry. It's easy to want other people to suffer for hurting me or someone I care about. It's hard to control my actions even when I know You'll take care of things. When I want to see someone punished, You want to show them love. You know their story. All I know is that they were rude. You have been kind to me. It shouldn't surprise me when You are kind to others. Help me trust Your decisions. Amen.

Stay away from every kind of evil.
1 Thessalonians 5:22 NLT

Dear God, You want me to respect Your protection. Sometimes it seems like there are too many things that You don't want me to do. It can be frustrating when I see other people do things You have told me to avoid. It could be that You are trying to protect me from bad influences, bad choices, and bad habits. You say no because You always have something better if I am just willing to wait, not because You don't want me to enjoy myself. Give me the courage to wait for Your best. Amen.

* * * * * * * * *

Children, obey your parents because you belong to the Lord, for this is the right thing to do.
Ephesians 6:1 NLT

Dear God, You say parents are pretty important. Self-control means making the choice to keep calm when it would be easy to lose my temper. I don't always agree with decisions my parents make. Your words say that obeying my parents is the right thing to do. I honor my parents because I want to be more like You. If it's important to You, then let it be important to me. Help me be kind in my responses and obedient in my actions, and let my face show Your joy. Amen.

> Those who are peacemakers will plant seeds
> of peace and reap a harvest of righteousness.
> JAMES 3:18 NLT

Dear God, You want me to be a farmer. I may never grow wheat or corn, but You want me to plant seeds of peace and harvest a crop of godly goodness. Self-control helps me become someone who helps others see the value of peacefulness. I don't like it when things are out of control, so help me be a peace farmer. You can water the peace seeds and help them grow. I can't wait to see Your crop of godly goodness. It should be a great harvest. Thanks for giving me the help I need. Amen.

* * * * * * * * *

> You must all be quick to listen, slow to speak,
> and slow to get angry.
> JAMES 1:19 NLT

Dear God, You never want me to say something I'll regret. Whenever I get angry, I either say or think things that are unkind. In Your words, You say I should listen more than I speak. There are times when what I want to say right away is not the same thing I would say if I waited. It's easy to get angry. It's easy to say the first thing I think. If I don't have self-control, I will never bring honor to You. Please help me control my tongue. Amen.

> Be careful how you live. Don't live like fools,
> but like those who are wise.
> EPHESIANS 5:15 NLT

Dear God, You don't want me to act foolishly. That means You really care for me. You want me to be wise. That means You have a plan for me. I want to be careful in the way I reply to my family, in how I react to the things other people do, in how I return good actions for bad intentions. I want Your name to be important to everyone. When I choose self-control, I will not act foolishly. I bring honor to Your name when I am careful in how I respond. Let me be careful—and wise. Amen.

* * * * * * * * *

> God is not a God of disorder but of peace.
> 1 CORINTHIANS 14:33 NLT

Dear God, You want our world to make sense. To do that You created day and night. You also created spring, summer, autumn, and winter. Everything You created works exactly as You wanted—except for people. You let us make choices. Sometimes we don't choose very well. We make a lot of really bad decisions. When we are self-controlled, we agree to cooperate with You in making peace from chaos. I want my decisions to make sense. I want to understand Your plans for me. I want to help other people see that a choice to follow You brings peace. Amen.

Don't love money; be satisfied with what you have. For God has said, "I will never fail you. I will never abandon you."
HEBREWS 13:5 NLT

Dear God, You want me to understand that You are more important than money. Sometimes that's hard to understand. I've seen things money can buy. There are many things I want, and I need money to buy them. But You are God. You created every animal, the oceans, sunrises, air, and flowers. You never charge for any of it. In fact, You give me eyes to see and a brain to remember their beauty. Gifts of love, joy, and peace are things money can't buy. Help me always to be satisfied with Your gifts. Amen.

MY TIME—
THE POWER OF PRIORITIES

You only get twenty-four hours to spend each day. You don't get more hours, minutes, or seconds, and you don't get less. You can only make decisions about the time you actually have.

Most people will spend seven to nine hours sleeping. Then there is the time you take to eat, take a shower, decide what to wear, attend school, do homework, and talk with parents and friends. In the time that's left, you can make decisions about how those hours and minutes are used.

Saying you'd spend that time with God is a great decision, but how exactly will you do it? God's words tell us there are many things He wants us to spend time developing. God doesn't leave us to guess.

You could spend time on your phone, the computer, and a video game, or you could discover the things that God says are really important. By discovering God's priority list, you can begin to spend time wisely.

Don't copy the behavior and customs of this world, but let God transform you into a new person by changing the way you think. Then you will learn to know God's will for you, which is good and pleasing and perfect.

ROMANS 12:2 NLT

Dear God, You say change is a good thing. You want me to be more different tomorrow that I am today. Once upon a time, I acted like a two-year-old. I've grown up since then. If I acted like I was still two years old, people would think something was wrong with me. I can learn to understand what You want me to do, but I need to grow up as a Christian. Please change the way I think, give me wisdom, and keep me away from the dumb stuff that keeps me from growing up. Amen.

> "Seek the Kingdom of God above all else, and live righteously, and he will give you everything you need."
> MATTHEW 6:33 NLT

Dear God, You have given me one priority that is above all others: seeking You is more important than anything else I can do. That means I need to make sure You are the most important part of my life. To spend time with You might mean I spend less time with hobbies, friends, and activities. It might mean I choose a time every day that I can spend reading Your words and praying. It means doing things differently so I can live life differently. You've given me everything I need to seek You. Thanks. Amen.

* * * * * * * * *

> "Wherever your treasure is, there the desires of your heart will also be."
> LUKE 12:34 NLT

Dear God, You gave me truth about why priorities are important. I will always spend my time on the things I believe are the most valuable. If I make sports the most important thing, then that's where I will want to spend my time. That's true with friendships, family, and fun. No one wants to spend too much time doing something they don't think is worthwhile. I want my greatest treasure to be my highest priority. I want to know You so well that spending time with You is what I really want to do most. Amen.

"Have no gods other than Me."
EXODUS 20:3 NLV

Dear God, You want me to follow You on purpose. You don't want me to view anything else as more important. My priority needs to be You. I can choose TV, sleep, hobbies, sports, music, friends, texting, or even food as a priority. These can be good things that become more important than You. Anything that's more important than You is like a god. Your words tell us not to follow other gods. Help me honor You above anything else I might enjoy. Amen.

* * * * * * * * *

Jesus replied, " 'You must love the Lord your God with all your heart, all your soul, and all your mind.' This is the first and greatest commandment."
MATTHEW 22:37–38 NLT

Dear God, You told me to love You, which sounds easy. After all, You are the Creator of all cool stuff. I can't go anywhere without seeing Your creativity. Why is it easy to appreciate what You've made and forget to appreciate You? If I'm supposed to love You, then I need to know You. That means more than understanding that You create sunsets, crickets, and ocean waves. If I'm supposed to love You with all my heart, soul, and mind, then help me look beyond what You created and discover You. Your words always have the answers. Thanks. Amen.

Teach us to realize the brevity of life, so that we may grow in wisdom.
PSALM 90:12 NLT

Dear God, You've given me time to become wise. Help me learn from You. Wisdom is a priority because without it I have no idea how to follow You. I could sing songs about You and feel good about the fact that You exist, but without wisdom I'm not sure what else I'm supposed to do. Eternity is forever, but each day is an opportunity to learn more about the One who lives in eternity. Because I don't understand everything about You, please make me wise. Help me learn something awesome today. Amen.

* * * * * * * * *

The Lord has told you what is good, and this is what he requires of you: to do what is right, to love mercy, and to walk humbly with your God.
MICAH 6:8 NLT

Dear God, You have given me three requirements that should be priorities in my life. You want me to do the right thing. You want me to be compassionate. You want me to respectfully follow where You lead. Each of these priorities means that I do what You ask, and You will always ask me to care for other people. If I follow You, I will find people who need compassion. In those moments, please help me to do the right thing. Your words tell me this is good, and I believe it is. Amen.

Don't worry about anything; instead, pray about everything.
Tell God what you need, and thank him for all he has done.
Then you will experience God's peace, which exceeds anything
we can understand. His peace will guard your hearts
and minds as you live in Christ Jesus.
PHILIPPIANS 4:6–7 NLT

Dear God, You created the priority of contentment. To be content
means I'm happy with what I have. When I'm content, I have
peace. When I'm not content, I worry. Worry makes me ask a
lot of "what if" questions. What if things get harder? What if I
look foolish when I sing in choir? What if I don't catch the ball?
Contentment helps me enjoy living because I already know You
love me in hard times, when I struggle to sing, and when I can't
catch a ball. Still, You accept me. Amen.

Whoever pursues righteousness and unfailing love
will find life, righteousness, and honor.
PROVERBS 21:21 NLT

Dear God, You've sent me on a journey, but instead of offering a pot of gold at the end of a rainbow, You offer three gifts: life, righteousness, and honor. To find these three gifts, I need to chase after righteousness and unfailing love. The only place I find those things is in You. Help me build endurance so I can be patient in my journey. Help me build obedience so I can bring You honor. Help me love You so I can really understand the life You want for me. I can't do any of these things without Your help. Amen.

* * * * * * * *

"Don't store up treasures here on earth, where moths eat them
and rust destroys them, and where thieves break in and steal.
Store your treasures in heaven, where moths and rust cannot
destroy, and thieves do not break in and steal."
MATTHEW 6:19–20 NLT

Dear God, You want decisions about my future to be a priority. Nothing seems to last forever. Trees die, riverbanks fall into the water, and things that are really valuable sometimes get stolen. Your words say that my greatest treasures are in heaven and they're completely safe. They won't be destroyed and nobody can steal them. My treasures there are different than here. Instead of money or collections, my treasure is You and all the changes You've made in family, my friends, and me. These are the treasures I want to see in heaven. Amen.

Pursue righteous living, faithfulness, love, and peace. Enjoy the companionship of those who call on the Lord with pure hearts.
2 TIMOTHY 2:22 NLT

Dear God, You want me to know I'm not alone in following Your directions for my life. Your words say that living in a way that brings honor to You, being loyal to You, giving and receiving Your love, and living peacefully with others are all priorities. More than just priorities, these traits help me want to be with other Christians who also follow You. When these priorities are important to me, I really can begin to see that I'm not the only one who wants to live differently—for You. Amen.

* * * * * * * * *

Let us come boldly to the throne of our gracious God. There we will receive his mercy, and we will find grace to help us when we need it most.
HEBREWS 4:16 NLT

Dear God, You want me to know that You are approachable. This can be hard to understand. You are awesome, and there is no one like You and never will be. I am amazed that I can come to You even when I sin. You promise to forgive me when I don't deserve it, and You offer me something better even though I didn't earn it. You call these two gifts mercy and grace. Your words say these are things I will need, and I have needed them often. Thanks for being approachable. Amen.

(Jesus said,) "I am giving you a new commandment: Love each other. Just as I have loved you, you should love each other. Your love for one another will prove to the world that you are my disciples."
JOHN 13:34–35 NLT

Dear God, You say that being an example of Your love should be a priority for me. I know that loving You is important, but loving others can be harder because they aren't perfect. Maybe that's one of the lessons of love. A person doesn't have to be perfect to need or give love. If everyone waited for other people to be perfect to love them, then there wouldn't be much compassion. I will make loving others a priority. My loving may not be perfect, but I will do it because I want to obey You with all my heart. Amen.

* * * * * * * *

Let us offer through Jesus a continual sacrifice of praise to God, proclaiming our allegiance to his name.
HEBREWS 13:15 NLT

Dear God, You have made honor a powerful priority. Your words say that I am to honor my parents and those who are in charge, like teachers, Sunday school leaders, police officers, and government officials. Even more than You want me to honor people in authority, You want me to honor You. I should make sure You know I plan to follow Your path for the rest of my life. There is no one greater than You, and I am in awe that I get to be Your child. You are worthy of praise, and I am just getting started. Amen.

I urge you, first of all, to pray for all people. Ask God to help them; intercede on their behalf, and give thanks for them. Pray this way for kings and all who are in authority so that we can live peaceful and quiet lives marked by godliness and dignity.

1 TIMOTHY 2:1–2 NLT

Dear God, You want me to prioritize the privilege of prayer. Some of the prayers You want me to pray are for others. I should pray for the wisdom I need, and when I do I will understand that I can help others by asking You to help them. I can thank You for the people You introduce me to. I can pray for wisdom for leaders who have hard decisions to make. When I am unselfish in how I pray, You have the opportunity to respond to my prayers. Thanks for the priority of unselfish prayer. Amen.

MY WORLD—
THE POWER OF COMPASSION

If you want to show compassion, just do what Jesus did. It's easy to understand. Jesus fed people who were hungry, gave water to people who were thirsty, prayed for the hurting, and stood up for those who needed a friend.

There are additional words that are part of the *compassion* family. You might think of words like *kindness, mercy, grace, caring, thoughtfulness, gentleness,* and *helpfulness.*

If you show compassion, you're giving something you don't expect to be returned. You choose kindness even when others are unkind. You make the decision to be thoughtful when others are not. You're gentle even when someone makes fun of you.

If you continually show compassion when others are unkind, they will begin to see that there is more power in your compassion than in their rudeness. It's hard to dislike someone who really cares about you.

If you want to see what compassion looks like, just look in the Bible. Compassion started with God. He remains compassionate even when we fail the kindness test.

All praise to God, the Father of our Lord Jesus Christ. God is our merciful Father and the source of all comfort. He comforts us in all our troubles so that we can comfort others. When they are troubled, we will be able to give them the same comfort God has given us.
2 CORINTHIANS 1:3–4 NLT

Dear God, You are a perfect example of compassion. You comfort me when I'm scared and help me when I need support. You know I need compassion. You also know I need to see what Your compassion looks like because You want me to show it to other people. You are the example I need to do what You ask me to do. You never leave me guessing what it looks like to choose Your way. I just need to spend time reading Your words so I know what You have said in order to do what You ask. Amen.

> Share each other's burdens, and in this way obey the law of Christ.
> **GALATIANS 6:2** NLT

Dear God, You want me to share, but not always the way I think. I know You want me to share what I have. I know You want me to share my time with others. Your words say I should share in the things that make other people sad, too. When I help others endure the hard things they face, I move a little closer to true compassion. Help me share. Amen.

* * * * * * * *

> So now there is no condemnation
> for those who belong to Christ Jesus.
> **ROMANS 8:1** NLT

Dear God, Your compassion is a gift to those who believe in You. Compassion can mean helping someone when they need help, but it can also mean forgiving someone when they could be condemned or found guilty of breaking Your law. When I believed that Jesus was Your Son and that when He died on the cross He was the perfect sacrifice to pay the price for breaking Your law, You offered me compassion. I am no longer guilty, because Jesus set me free from sin's payment. Help me to offer my obedience in return. Amen.

The faithful love of the LORD never ends! His mercies never cease.
Great is his faithfulness; his mercies begin afresh each morning.
LAMENTATIONS 3:22—23 NLT

Dear God, Your compassion never expires. Your love never ends.
Your mercies extend beyond the horizon. You cover me with a
blanket of protection shielding me from the harsh conditions
I face. I will deal with problems. In fact, Your words tell me I
am guaranteed trouble, but You walk with me, You show Your
love before, during, and after I face a challenge. I never have to
handle hurt alone. You are always with me showing love that
never changes and never goes away. Help me stay close to that
compassionate love. Amen.

* * * * * * * *

You, O Lord, are a God of compassion and mercy, slow to get
angry and filled with unfailing love and faithfulness.
PSALM 86:15 NLT

Dear God, You'd rather forgive than get angry. That is different
than the way I sometimes feel. For me it's easier to get angry first
and then think about whether I want to forgive the person who
made me mad. When I think about it, I always like the feeling
when anger goes away. If I forgive first, I don't have to live through
the frustration of being mad. You choose mercy. You decide on
compassion. You hand out love more easily than free samples at
the store. You're God, and that's why I follow You. Amen.

Love each other with genuine affection,
and take delight in honoring each other.
ROMANS 12:10 NLT

Dear God, You really want me to love people, not just act like I do. If anybody knows the difference, it's You. Sometimes when I want to win, it can be hard to congratulate the actual winner, yet that's what You want. More than just a change in choice, You want to change my heart so I can really love and honor people. When I think I'm the only one who should win, I'm not really showing compassion for others. I should always do my best but always rejoice with those who need it. Keep working on me. Amen.

* * * * * * * * *

Love is patient and kind. Love is not jealous or boastful or proud.
1 CORINTHIANS 13:4 NLT

Dear God, Your words tell me what love is, and it's not a feeling. Compassionate love is willing to wait, it trusts, and it is modest and humble. I know there's more to love than this, but I can decide to wait. I can trust and be modest. I don't even have to point out my good qualities to other people—and it's a choice. If I feel good about it afterward, then maybe that's a bonus. It's a decision You can help me with. Because You choose to love me, help me follow. Amen.

Let all that I am praise the LORD; may I never forget the good things he does for me. He forgives all my sins and heals all my diseases. He redeems me from death and crowns me with love and tender mercies.
PSALM 103:2–4 NLT

Dear God, Your compassion changes something inside me. When I want to thank You, all I have to do is think back at all the things You've done for me. You created this world, my family, eyes, ears, friends, joy, peace, and love. You give me life, forgive my sin, heal my hurts, and make sure there's plenty of love and mercy for me to appreciate. You do *all* this—for me. Whenever I need to understand why compassion is important, I just need to remember You and I can't help but praise. You're amazing, God. Amen.

> People who conceal their sins will not prosper, but if they confess and turn from them, they will receive mercy.
> PROVERBS 28:13 NLT

Dear God, You want my heart to be clean. I can't clean it myself, which is why You want me to be honest about what I've done. You want to hear about the good things. You want to show compassion in my struggles. My sins are also important to You. It isn't because You want to punish, but because You want to remove my sin so I can get back to growing up. You want my permission to clean my heart, so help me share the good, bad, and lawbreaking parts of my life with You. Thanks for forgiveness. Amen.

* * * * * * * * *

> Kind words are like honey—sweet to the soul and healthy for the body.
> PROVERBS 16:24 NLT

Dear God, You really understand people. You know I like it when people are kind. Your words say that if kindness were food, then it would be the sweetest thing around. Even though it's sweet, it's still healthy for me. Sometimes things that are good for me don't taste great, so this is awesome. Your words even say that speaking kind words is healthy for the body. More people should know about the healthy sweetness of being kind. Help me spread the word. Amen.

A gentle answer deflects anger, but harsh words make tempers flare.
PROVERBS 15:1 NLT

Dear God, there are some things You don't want me to do if my goal is to be compassionate. I have been motivated to be kind to others because You've been a perfect role model. But Your words tell me that everyone can make bad choice when they're angry. You say I can help others avoid being angry by using compassionate ways to reply even when being angry would be easier. If anger is like a wildfire, then please use the way I respond to help put out the flames. Amen.

* * * * * * * *

Encourage each other and build each other up,
just as you are already doing.
1 THESSALONIANS 5:11 NLT

Dear God, You want to use me to encourage other people. It's easy to feel as if my best is never good enough. All the decorating I can do to a kiddie pool doesn't change the fact it's just a kiddie pool. I've seen what You've done with a lake. Now that's impressive. When I feel like a failure, it's easy to believe that other people do, too. You want me to help my family, friends, and neighbors to see they can always do more when they accept Your help. I want to be that kind of encouragement. Amen.

Your kindness will reward you, but your cruelty will destroy you.
PROVERBS 11:17 NLT

Dear God, You tell me I'll be rewarded for being kind. You say that being mean will crush me. Since no one has given me a kindness award and I haven't been destroyed for being mean, You must have a different way for me to understand Your words. Compassion helps others and it helps me. Being cruel hurts others and it hurts me. Even if I have to wait, I'm always better off when I choose Your guidance over how I feel. Being mean makes my heart and mind twisted and ugly. Help me to remember the true rewards of compassion. Amen.

* * * * * * * * *

Whenever we have the opportunity, we should do good to everyone—especially to those in the family of faith.
GALATIANS 6:10 NLT

Dear God, You want my life to be a billboard for compassion. You want my heart to give gentleness a leadership role. You want me to go into business with kindness. You say that caring for others is an opportunity. You even say that compassion is a great response that should be given to those who follow You. Being like Jesus is hard because I have sinned and I'm not perfect. Help me pay attention to those times when You give me an opportunity to show compassion to others. Help me do what I know You'd want. Amen.

Oh, the joys of those who are kind to the poor! The LORD rescues them when they are in trouble. The LORD protects them and keeps them alive.
PSALM 41:1–2 NLT

Dear God, You want me to be kind to people who struggle. You are kind to me, and I struggle. Now I get it. You always want me to do what You do. You love me, so I should love others. You show me mercy, so I should do the same thing. You rescue people in trouble, and You rescued me when I was in trouble. Sometimes I make things harder than I should. You don't ask me to do something You haven't already done. When I do what You do, You promise the gift of joy. Thanks, God. Amen.

MY WORRY—
THE POWER OF PEACE

Have you ever wondered why you worry? Maybe you're afraid of what might occur, but your mind can think of all kinds of bad situations that make it worse.

You might think worrying over a problem will help the problem go away, but it just wastes time and energy on something you can't change or control.

You may know that God understands all things and wants to develop a plan for a good outcome, but you struggle with anxiety. When you worry, you act as if God is too small to take care of the things He actually controls.

The worry you decide to think about may be yours, but God wants to take it from you and replace it with peace. When your mind and heart are peaceful, there's not much room for worry. On the other hand, when your heart and mind are worried, there's not much room for peace.

Let God take the things you worry about. It's not a burden for Him. He already knows how the story ends. Maybe that's why He isn't worried, and you shouldn't be, either.

For peace to grow, show worry the door.

(Jesus said,) "I am leaving you with a gift—peace of mind and heart. And the peace I give is a gift the world cannot give. So don't be troubled or afraid."

JOHN 14:27 NLT

Dear God, when it comes to worry, Your replacement gift is peace, which is different than thinking of a world that doesn't need soldiers. Your peace is my being confident that You can take care of anything I could possibly worry about. Life can still be hard, but Your peace means that no matter how bad things get, I don't need to be afraid because You're big enough to manage all the worry in the world. Amen.

> In peace I will lie down and sleep, for you alone,
> O LORD, will keep me safe.
> PSALM 4:8 NLT

Dear God, You work the night shift so I can sleep in peace. Your words tell me that You made me. I can be like You by making choices that You would make, but I am nothing like You, because while You're perfect, I sin. You don't need sleep, but I do. When I lay down to sleep, help me to remember that You watch over me. You want the best for me, and the absolutely best gift when I need to sleep is peace. Your gifts make me thankful. Amen.

* * * * * * * * *

> Look at those who are honest and good, for a wonderful future
> awaits those who love peace.
> PSALM 37:37 NLT

Dear God, You want me to chase after peace, because Your words say that a "wonderful future awaits those who love peace." Even if there was no promise of a wonderful future, I'd love Your peace more than my chaos. To have peace means worry can't find a place to rest in my heart. To have peace means my face shows joy more than fear. To have peace means anger is less likely to come between friendships. I love Your peace. Help me to keep peace as a permanent change in the way I live and in how I respond. Amen.

May the Lord of peace himself give you his peace at all times
and in every situation.
2 THESSALONIANS 3:16 NLT

Dear God, Your words call You the Lord of peace. This special name helps me understand that You want peace to overflow in my life like a waterfall. You want me to accept Your peace in every situation I face. Help me stay away from drama that distracts me from Your peace. Help me encourage others to accept Your peace. Help me love Your peace enough to accept it instead of hugging the hurtful choice of worry. Help me find a home within Your peace so that when bad days come, my heart is at home with You. Amen.

* * * * * * * * *

When I am afraid, I will put my trust in you. I praise God for what
he has promised. I trust in God, so why should I be afraid?
PSALM 56:3—4 NLT

Dear God, Your promises make trusting You much easier. Every time I'm afraid of all the things that might happen, You want me to think of all the things You have promised. You want me to see that Your words are filled with promises that have already been kept. You have always been worth trusting. You've always taken care of those who follow You. Help me remember the things You have done, and then help me to remember to say thanks. Worry and fear can't compare to trust and praise. Keep reminding me of Your promises. Amen.

When doubts filled my mind, your comfort
gave me renewed hope and cheer.
PSALM 94:19 NLT

Dear God, You bring the greatest hope, the most joyous cheer, and the comfort I need when *doubt* drops by with friends. Sometimes I try to be brave and confident. I try to convince myself and other people that I never have doubts, but I think I do a very bad job of being confident. I can doubt that my friends like me, that I'm ready for a test, or that I will ever be good at anything. I need Your comfort, hope, and cheer. Let me never doubt Your love. Amen.

* * * * * * * * *

(Jesus said,) "Here on earth you will have many trials and sorrows.
But take heart, because I have overcome the world."
JOHN 16:33 NLT

Dear God, if life is a battle between good and evil, You win. I would love to live in a world where life is easy, people are kind, and bad things don't happen to good people. I don't live in this kind of world. Since each person gets to make choices, I might get sad because some of their decisions will make things difficult for me. When worry comes knocking, I can send him away without inviting him in because You have overcome the power of sinful choices. Thanks for being my Defender. Amen.

Be still in the presence of the LORD, and wait patiently for him
to act. Don't worry about evil people who prosper
or fret about their wicked schemes.
PSALM 37:7 NLT

Dear God, You need me to be patient while I wait for Your answers.
Sometimes I worry about whether You'll answer, how You'll
answer, and when the answer will come. This happens especially
when I think about other people who seem to be rewarded for
doing the wrong thing. When I notice myself worrying about
the bad decisions other people make, You ask me to stop and
wait patiently for you to take care of things at the right time. You
promise to take care of things. I'm sure glad You can handle that.
I'd be exhausted just trying. Thanks. Amen.

(Jesus said,) "Don't let your hearts be troubled.
Trust in God, and trust also in me."
JOHN 14:1 NLT

Dear God, how did You know I had trouble trusting? Well, I
suppose it's because You're God and You know everything. Since
You know everything, it makes sense that Your words tell me never
to allow my heart to become worried. When I worry, I find it hard
to believe that anyone can handle what I go through except me.
Then again, I never really handle things well when I worry, and I
either forget or refuse to let You handle my troubles. Remind me
often that I need to trust You. Amen.

* * * * * * * *

Give your burdens to the LORD, and he will take care of you.
He will not permit the godly to slip and fall.
PSALM 55:22 NLT

Dear God, You want my "worry" backpack to be empty. I know
I don't really have a worry backpack, but it can seem like it. The
more worry I carry the heavier it seems to get. The heavier it is, the
harder it is for me to find joy. The harder it is to find joy, the sadder
I become. The sadder I am, the harder it is to follow You. If I worry
less, then I can follow You more. When You take care of me, I can
enjoy walking with You. Help me walk—without worry. Amen.

Worry weighs a person down;
an encouraging word cheers a person up.
PROVERBS 12:25 NLT

Dear God, You send people to help me remember who You are.
These friends are like a life vest for someone who can't swim very
well. They help keep my head above water by sharing helpful
words when I'm weary from worry. These are good friends to
have, and they are examples of the kind of friend I want to be. You
created each of us to be able to give gifts of encouraging words.
Each of us needs support. Help me trust You and encourage others
to give trust a try. Amen.

* * * * * * * * *

Then Jesus said, "Come to me, all of you who are weary and carry
heavy burdens, and I will give you rest."
MATTHEW 11:28 NLT

Dear God, You want me to get a good night's rest. I wake up in the
middle of the night and I'm worried about a lot of stuff. It could be
whether the front door is locked or whether I did all my homework.
I roll around like a rotisserie chicken. I don't get any rest, and I'm
usually grouchy in the morning. I worry about big things, small
things, and some in the middle of the worry scale. Because I'm
weary, You ask me to bring my sack of assorted burdens to You.
That sounds really good. I'm tired. Amen.

Give all your worries and cares to God, for he cares about you.
1 PETER 5:7 NLT

Dear God, You want me to give You the worst possible gift, and getting rid of it is for my own good. Worries are things I hang on to because I think really bad stuff will happen. My mind can take off in a dozen directions, I can't sleep or concentrate, and my joy is in hibernation. Your words say You care about me and You can take care of any worry that introduces itself to me. It doesn't seem like the greatest gift, but since You want it, help me give worry a new home with You. Amen.

* * * * * * * * *

"Can all your worries add a single moment to your life?"
MATTHEW 6:27 NLT

Dear God, You have a question, and You want an answer. Can worry make me live longer? The answer is no. Worry *has* taken time away from really living because instead of spending moments with people I love, I spend them worrying about things I can't control. Why do I do that? Right now it doesn't make sense to hold on to worry, but I will probably worry again, and each second I refuse to let You handle things is another second I will struggle with trust. Help me remember You are faithful to take care of me. Amen.

Those who trust in the LORD will find new strength. They will soar high on wings like eagles. They will run and not grow weary. They will walk and not faint.
ISAIAH 40:31 NLT

Dear God, Your words tell me how I can be strong. You want my life to demonstrate that I can endure difficult times. My strength comes from You. I grow stronger when I trust and weaker when I worry. Your words say I can move forward without worry and without being exhausted. Help me make the brave choice to trust You with every worry. I don't have to spend time struggling to know that You're the right One to handle any trouble. The minute I spot worry, let me run to You—and drop it off. Amen.

SCRIPTURE INDEX